WHAT ARE YOU CHASING Y

What's the point? What is life's purpose, and how do you build faith

about an invisible God who can be hard to understand? We grow

weary under the weight of such questions, walking through our days

feeling inadequate and tired from what feels like the heavy burden of

a religion of rules. A lifetime of striving and wrestling with doubts

has been quieted as I've studied the book in the Bible known as

Esther.

Once chained by the sense that I was never enough and missing that

only Jesus is enough, I've been set free from a prison of my own

making. I want my freedom to lead you to the way out as well. I owe

that to you. I cannot walk out of these prisons without showing those

left behind how to find the way of escape.

If you want to feel the freedom of walking in the unforced rhythms of

grace (Matthew 11:28-31, The Message), then let's be wrecked

together by the story in Esther. Here we will find the unfathomable story of the triune God and how he changes and equips us with all that we need for the kingdom of endless grace.

Because he is enough.

CHASE THE KINGDOM:

Finding Purpose Through

the Book of Esther

Heather Enright

Published through KDP, Kindle Direct Publishing, a subsidiary of Amazon.

ISBN 9781688028906.   *Printed in the United States of America*

"If we find ourselves with a desire
that nothing in this world can satisfy,
the most probable explanation is
that we were made for another world."

— C.S. Lewis

CONTENTS

Prologue to the Book of Esther

Tucked within the Old Testament, we find the improbable story of a teenage girl named Esther. The biblical book of Esther vividly portrays the triune God and the truth of the gospel, although it's the only book in the Bible that never mentions God's name. Who, but God, reveals his character and his loving plan for us without his name ever being uttered?

Before we journey through this fascinating book about the kingdom of God, let's consider the backstory. Esther is one of the five books of the Megillot; meaning, it's one of the five books or scrolls that are grouped together in Jewish tradition. The events recorded within the book of Esther is where the Jewish feast of Purim originates.

The historical timing of the book of Esther is from 483 BC until 472 BC. Esther is believed to have been fourteen years old at the time that she became queen. The Talmud, or Jewish law and legend, cites Mordecai as the author of Esther. Mordecai was the relative, noted to be her cousin, who raised Esther after she was orphaned. Esther's father was Abihail from the tribe of Benjamin, and her family is traditionally believed to be part of the Jewish population that was carried into Babylonian exile from their beloved home in Jerusalem.

Within the history of the Israelite nation, the life of Esther came after the Egyptian captivity and the forty years of desert wandering with Moses until God brought his people to the promised land of Canaan under Joshua's leadership. Once settled in this land of promise, the Israelites began to flip-flop from obedience to God to the worship of idols.

As prophesied, the Israelites were taken into captivity in Babylon after the fall of the city of Jerusalem because of their divided hearts toward God. Babylon is the setting where we find the account of Shadrach, Meshach, and Abednego being thrown into the fiery furnace after they refused to bow to King Nebuchadnezzar. Babylon is also where Daniel was thrown into the lion's den. Both of these accounts are written in the Old Testament book of Daniel, which chronologically occurred before Esther's story.

Historians report that Babylon fell in 539 BC under King Cyrus. The next year the Jews were allowed to pursue rebuilding the temple as some returned to Jerusalem to restore the temple altar and foundation. Temple work halted under the next king, Cambyses, who reigned from 530 BC to 522 BC. In 520 to 519 BC, King Darius became king and rediscovered Cyrus' edict for temple rebuilding, which was then completed during the sixth year of Darius' reign.

King Ahasuerus, also called Xerxes in some Bible translations, became king after Darius in 486 BC. The pronunciation of Ahasuerus is *uh*-haz-yoo-**eer**-*uh* s, or as I have broken it down by listening, *uh-has-you-ERR-us*.₁ Ahasuerus ruled over a large region from Southwest Asia to the Middle East, including lands from India to Ethiopia. During his reign, his kingdom struggled to maintain power over the Greeks.

As exiles in this vast kingdom, the Jewish people were living among mysticism and a variety of belief systems. During the life of Esther, King Ahasuerus ruled from his winter palace and the surrounding city, known as the citadel of Susa, which was located over 980 miles from Jerusalem.

Although Cyrus had allowed the Jews to go back to rebuild the temple many years prior, the great distance served as just one of the obstacles. Many Jews had acclimated to life in exile and knew nothing else. Therefore, at the time of Esther's life, the Jews were scattered throughout the kingdom that Ahasuerus ruled over.

King Ahasuerus was assassinated in 465 BC, and his son, Artaxerxes, took the throne in Susa. He was served by a Jewish cupbearer named Nehemiah. The book of Nehemiah, though placed before Esther in the Old Testament, recounts events that occurred after Esther was queen. In Nehemiah 2:6, we find reference to the queen who sat by the king during Nehemiah's request to go rebuild the walls and city of Jerusalem. Jewish scholars debate whether this noted queen is Esther. Nevertheless, most experts agree that given the overlap of Esther's life and the life of her assumed stepson, Artaxerxes, Esther had some amount of influence over the decision to both allow Nehemiah to go back to Jerusalem and to also offer provisions for the rebuilding efforts. In regard to the provisions, some believe that one-third of Haman's estate, which was granted to Esther and Mordecai in Esther chapter 8, was used toward Nehemiah's rebuilding funds. 2

While reading and researching Esther and the background of her story, I've found her to be an outsider and an unlikely central figure in God's plans for his people. She was a woman in a male-dominant culture who was also an orphaned Jewess from the smallest of the tribes of Israel, living in exile. During her life, we see Esther come to experience privilege and status in the midst of comparison and competition. She was commanded to deny her true identity and faith, masquerading the secret of who she really was. Then, at a critical moment, she had to decide if she was willing to risk everything, including her life, to chase the kingdom of God rather than the kingdom in front of her.

We, like Esther, face the challenge of embracing our identity and purpose in an unseen kingdom while struggling behind masks in this kingdom of here and now.

The most quoted verse from the book of Esther, often seen on coffee cups and t-shirts, comes from Esther 4:14 as Mordecai pleads with his beloved Esther. He asks her, "… And who knows but that you have come to royal position for such a time as this?"

We, like Esther, stand at a place of decision while staring down our future. Let us, therefore, not forget the first half of Esther 4:14, which holds the verse's pivotal guiding truth.

Mordecai utters this question to Esther only after he has confidently declared that God will deliver and rescue his people. The question isn't what Esther will accomplish, but, rather, if she will participate in what God promises to do with or without her. The wonder of Esther 4:14 isn't that Esther was to embrace her place and position, but rather that our Sovereign and Omnipotent God would be so audacious as to invite any of us to partner with his kingdom plans. I thank you for taking this journey into Esther as we consider how to center our life's pursuits around our identity as defined by the gospel of God. This is what I've written in my prayer journal for each of you readers as we learn about God through the story of Esther:

Come and hear, all you who fear God;

let me tell you what he has done for me.

I cried out to him with my mouth;

his praise was on my tongue.

If I had cherished sin in my heart,

the Lord would not have listened;

but God has surely listened and has heard my prayer.

Praise be to God,

who has not rejected my prayer

or withheld his love from me!

Psalm 66:16-20 (NIV)

May we quit chasing the kingdom in front of us and its tiresome demands of status and approval. May we abandon our efforts to be good church girls earning our way to heaven. May we lay down our heavy burdens and run unencumbered, confident that he is the God of rescue and deliverance, freedom and healing.

This is the time. Do you want to get well?

Introduction to Esther

The Question

"Do you want to get well?"

In the Gospel of John chapter 5, Jesus asks this question of the invalid man who had been lying by the pool of Bethesda for thirty-eight years.

Do you want to get well?

To be honest, this initially struck me as a ridiculous question to ask a man who had spent nearly four decades with suffering and immobility. Yet the man avoided directly answering the simple question, instead explaining that no one helped him, and other people always beat him to the pool when the waters were stirred offering physical healing.

When Jesus poses this question, he's probing beyond the man's physical ailments.

Do you want to get well?

Do you want more than these paralyzed places?

Do you want to keep on in the familiar kingdom of current circumstances and in the dissatisfaction of the counterfeit and empty?

Or do you want more?

Do you want to rise up beyond the immobility of past wounds, legalistic living, and a shallow faith?

Do you want to float in the deep pools of grace, confident that you are both fully known and fully loved?

Or will you keep being tossed by the waves of man's approval and life's circumstance?

These are the questions I've been asking myself for the last few years. I've spent decades chasing who I thought Jesus was, with a divided heart, bowing to the idol of self, and seeking my own comfort and glory. In fact, I've spent my entire life in church pews, longing for a soul-felt freedom beyond an occasional and brief emotional high. I've spent years feeling rather smug about my "good girl" life in the church and coddling a "me and them" mentality, where "others" were the real sinners. Self-righteousness is a rather deceptive thing, taking root easily, growing wildly, and convincing us that we are fine as we are.

Three years ago, I found myself paralyzed by rejections, circumstances, and depression. In the bustle of life and the lies of social media, I found myself living like this invalid man, lying around, waiting for someone to fix things. I was waiting for someone to save me with their validation of my worth and importance. I was waiting to be invited back to the tables where I had been left out. I felt a profound loneliness and a fragility that made social settings a scary place. It felt as though someone else always got there before me, denying me my chance at approval. I was living from a scarcity mentality, believing there's only so much to go around and someone else's gain meant I lost.

But the Savior asked, "Do you want to get well?"

In a million tiny ways, he asked me to rise up and carry my mat to walk out of it. It came slowly to this stubborn girl, but as friendships and positions were stripped away, I found myself sitting for long hours with my Bible and prayer journal. It was desperation initially, with the warped thinking of, "I guess all I can do is pray." In his kindness, the three years of sitting and listening have moved me from lying by a Bethesda pool to rising up in a healing and a wholeness that I have never known.

The Answer

While sitting in my paralyzed places, I've been captivated by the book of Esther. Over and again, for ten years, God has brought me back to Esther. While peeling back the layers of this remarkable story, I've found a parallel of my own faith journey.

The first time through, I found Esther to be like a fairy tale about a cartoon princess, leaving me with warm fuzzies and superficial analysis about beauty and what God has to say about that.
The next time through, I dug deeper and found greater truths about who God calls us to be as daughters of the King. I found themes of modesty, kindness, and humility that informed me of how I should act.

On this note, allow me to offer an apology to the darling girls to whom I taught the book of Esther back then because I was teaching them primarily about themselves. This may not seem like a problem, except that the Bible is meant to tell us about God. In every story of the Bible, and in every study of it, God alone is the protagonist. The truth is that God cannot be the protagonist in our own life story until we build a belief that he alone is worthy of being the central character. A proper awe of God comes only when we realize our desperate ongoing need for him.

All my life, I've never strayed from following Jesus. I've failed countless times in any given hour of my life, but I've never walked away from trying to follow him. The dilemma was that I was chasing a faith of addition.

Jesus plus.

Jesus plus being a good girl.

Jesus plus being approved by others.

Jesus plus following the rules.

Jesus plus striving to earn my place in heaven.

Jesus plus all the other "good" things to make me feel happy and whole.

Jesus plus fighting against the waves of emotions and worries, tossed about by circumstances.

Success. Achievement. Status. Recognition.

I've spent my entire life following a Jesus I never truly understood. It's been a brutal and beautiful process to navigate this Great Awakening to grace. The big breakthrough came through a hard conversation.

I initially felt humiliated and defensive when a friend lovingly confronted me with blunt questions.

When will Jesus be enough? When will he plus nothing be enough to satisfy? To fulfill? To leave me full of continual hope and joy and peace that the Son of the Almighty God secured for me through his death and resurrection?

Hear me clearly. Lean in and listen.

I don't want you to waste a day of your life on a faith of addition. I don't want you to misunderstand the gospel story or ride the waves of a faith led by feelings because doing so denies the freedom Jesus gives.

If you're a mom like me, you've spent your adult life trying to raise "good Christian" kids. You've taken them to church and told them Bible stories and even attended Bible studies yourself. When you find yourself mothering teenagers, preparing to launch them from your nest, you wonder if you've done "enough."

A faith of striving drowns us and leaves us questioning if the faith we've passed on will stick. Maybe deep down the doubts arise from an internal dissatisfaction with a faith of addition, sensing its lack.

24

The reality in our social media, success-driven, and Christian cliché world is that we've lost, or maybe never discovered, a rightful wonder of the God of the universe.

Here's a diagnostic question on this subject. When you consider the cross, do you feel blessed about what a nice story it is that gave you a way to go to heaven? Is the cross an entrance ticket? Or is the cross the humbling center point of your thoughts, actions, and words? Do you feel a awe deep within you that continually makes you overcome with gratitude for what the perfect glorious King did for you? Does the gospel story make you ache for the day when Jesus rights all that's wrong and you see him face-to-face?

Similar to how Jesus questioned the invalid man, my pastor often poses two questions that cut me to the core.

First of all, do you have a problem extending grace to others or to yourself? If so, then you have a problem understanding the grace shown to you.1

Secondly, whose opinion matters most to you? Because "until the opinion of the One who matters most, matters most to you, you will never be free." [2]

We live in a world where the impossible standards are invading even the sacred territory of motherhood. I am of a generation that grew up with the idea of the Kool-Aid mom. Now, she creates elaborate gatherings with admirable themes, beautiful décor, and a menu of vegetables and fruit artfully displayed like a masterpiece. In our current culture, the Proverbs 31 woman is one who serves cuisine that is organic, GMO-free, gluten-free, dairy-free, and free of any appearance of mediocrity.

Our screens constantly tell us of the dangers of screen addiction. We are the pioneer parents in a digital age, and we, as moms, are ever throttling forward to "the moment." You know the one—it's the one people speak of in hushed tones as if a death is approaching. It's the moment when your offspring will be launched from your nest. You are staring this down, imagining that your children's peers are applying for college with an impressive resume of academic perfection, off-the-chart test scores, and active participation in a plethora of extracurricular activities, all while spending their summers building water wells in Africa.

There's a lot in this kingdom of here and now that deceives us about falling behind while we lie around immobilized and striving for what we cannot attain on our own. We become imprisoned by the yearning and working for more.

Are you chasing the kingdom of self, looking for comfort and accolades by doing good deeds?

Are you seeking the fleeting kingdom of popularity and ease and success?

Or are you chasing the kingdom of grace, where you are no longer bossed around by feelings and approval?

Do you want to get well?

Once chained by the sense that I was never enough and missing that only Jesus is enough, I've now been set free from a prison of my own making. I want my freedom to lead you to the way out as well. I owe that to you. I cannot walk out of these prisons without showing those left behind how to find the way of escape.

If you want to feel the freedom of walking in the unforced rhythms of grace (Matthew 10:28-31, *The Message*), then let's be wrecked together by the story in Esther. Here we will find the unfathomable story of the triune God and how he changes and equips us with all that we need for the kingdom of endless grace.

Because he is enough.

Author's note on how to study Esther:

The actual text of Esther is included within every chapter because my heart's desire is to see us read the Word of God rather than only books written about it. I pray every one of you is inspired with a deeper love and appreciation for the Bible as the guiding truth that stands on its own to instruct us.

In 2016, I developed a study method to help me better understand Scripture. You can cut out the following page to use as a bookmark and study tool for the text of Esther. I pray this will equip you to continue to read any passage of God's Word with fresh understanding and application. If you are prone to using colored pencils or highlighters, you might use a different color for each of the three reflection questions.

1—ADORATION

Read through the passage and consider what it reveals about God. Looking for these truths will teach our minds to think on the wonders of God's character.

As you read the verses, prayerfully consider these questions and look for the answers, highlighting the words or phrases in the biblical passage:

> • *What do these verses reveal about God, through both his*
> *actions and words? Or characters in the story that allude to him?*
> • *What do they tell me about his character and nature?*
> • *What do they tell me about how he interacts with his people?*

Now form these truths into sentences of adoration, which you can journal in a separate notebook. In the future, you can refer back to these praises to preach the truth of God to yourself.

Looking at your answers from above, fill in the blank:
> **You are the God who _____.**

2—AFFIRMATION

Read through the passage again to see what it reveals about our own identity because of God's love and Jesus' death and resurrection. Every passage of Scripture can shape our gospel identity.

Ask yourself these questions.
> • *What do these verses say about me and others as they describe God's people?*
> • *What do these verses tell me about how God sees me and acts toward me?*
> • *What do these verses promise me about who I am in God because of Jesus?*

Next, form these answers into sentences that affirm your gospel identity (and all of God's people) by filling in the blank:
> **I am _____.**

3—ACTION

Read the passage a third time and see how it calls you to respond. Every passage calls us to action. Reading God's Word should instruct our adoration of God, inform our identity before him, and stir us to think, speak, and act in ways that bring glory to him.

ESTHER 1

When these days were over, the king gave a banquet, lasting seven

days, in the enclosed garden of the king's palace, for all the people

from the least to the greatest...

Esther 1:5

"According to the law, what must be done...?"

Esther 1:15

Esther 1, *English Standard Version*

The King's Banquets

1 Now in the days of Ahasuerus, the Ahasuerus who reigned from India to Ethiopia over 127 provinces, 2 in those days when King Ahasuerus sat on his royal throne in Susa, the citadel, 3 in the third year of his reign he gave a feast for all his officials and servants. The army of Persia and Media and the nobles and governors of the provinces were before him, 4 while he showed the riches of his royal glory and the splendor and pomp of his greatness for many days, 180 days.5 And when these days were completed, the king gave for all the people present in Susa the citadel, both great and small, a feast lasting for seven days in the court of the garden of the king's palace. 6 There were white cotton curtains and violet hangings fastened with cords of fine linen and purple to silver rods and marble pillars, and also couches of gold and silver on a mosaic pavement of porphyry, marble, mother-of-pearl, and precious stones. 7 Drinks were served in golden vessels, vessels of different kinds, and the royal wine was lavished according to the bounty of the king. 8 And drinking was according to this edict: "There is no compulsion." For

34

the king had given orders to all the staff of his palace to do as each man desired. 9 Queen Vashti also gave a feast for the women in the palace that belonged to King Ahasuerus.

Queen Vashti's Refusal

10 On the seventh day, when the heart of the king was merry with wine, he commanded Mehuman, Biztha, Harbona, Bigtha and Abagtha, Zethar and Carkas, the seven eunuchs who served in the presence of King Ahasuerus, 11 to bring Queen Vashti before the king with her royal crown, in order to show the peoples and the princes her beauty, for she was lovely to look at. 12 But Queen Vashti refused to come at the king's command delivered by the eunuchs. At this the king became enraged, and his anger burned within him.

13 Then the king said to the wise men who knew the times (for this was the king's procedure toward all who were versed in law and judgment, 14 the men next to him being Carshena, Shethar, Admatha, Tarshish, Meres, Marsena, and Memucan, the seven princes of Persia and Media, who saw the king's face, and sat first in the kingdom): 15 "According to the law, what is to be done to Queen

Vashti, because she has not performed the command of King Ahasuerus delivered by the eunuchs?" 16 Then Memucan said in the presence of the king and the officials, "Not only against the king has Queen Vashti done wrong, but also against all the officials and all the peoples who are in all the provinces of King Ahasuerus.17 For the queen's behavior will be made known to all women, causing them to look at their husbands with contempt, since they will say, 'King Ahasuerus commanded Queen Vashti to be brought before him, and she did not come.' 18 This very day the noble women of Persia and Media who have heard of the queen's behavior will say the same to all the king's officials, and there will be contempt and wrath in plenty. 19 If it pleases the king, let a royal order go out from him, and let it be written among the laws of the Persians and the Medes so that it may not be repealed, that Vashti is never again to come before King Ahasuerus. And let the king give her royal position to another who is better than she. 20 So when the decree made by the king is proclaimed throughout all his kingdom, for it is vast, all women will give honor to their husbands, high and low alike." 21 This advice pleased the king and the princes, and the king did as Memucan proposed.22 He sent letters to all the royal provinces, to every province in its own script and to every people in its own language, that every man be master in his own household and speak according to the language of his people.

IF NOT FOR GOD

Esther 1

Growing up, I struggled to fit in. Being an Army brat meant moving every few years and the endless cycle of being the new girl. I'd attempt to settle in, figure out the routines at the new school, and evaluate the social scene. I always wanted to be included at the lunch table and invited to the birthday parties.

Just before eighth grade, we moved again. My dad made a huge leap from being an Army officer to becoming a pastor of a very small church in a tiny Texas town. This was no Army base where everyone was accustomed to moving in and out. These kids had known each other since birth. Their parents had known each other since birth. Their grandparents... well, you get the picture. This last stop for me before college felt like an uphill climb. How would I ever be accepted as "one of them"?

I managed to settle in a bit, joining various clubs in high school and forming friendships. But, to be perfectly honest, I never shook the feeling of being an outsider. I felt the full weight of this angst with the approach of the Junior and Senior Prom.

Listen, when your town doesn't have so much as a McDonald's or a movie theater, prom is a major social occasion. In that town, they celebrate prom like nowhere else. On prom night, all the couples line up to "promenade" up one side of the river, over the bridge, across the other side, and then back again. Parents, grandparents, and all manner of extended family line up with an array of cameras to snap photos and compare notes on what each girl is wearing.

You aren't just invited to prom to go to a dance. You are invited to be seen by the entire town. Lest you think your absence won't be noticed, such details are seldom overlooked in small-town Texas. Imagine my relief when an invitation was offered, and I knew that I, too, would join the ranks of my peers, walking up and down the sidewalks along the banks of the Lampasas River for all the townsfolk paparazzi. I can assure you that my bright, metallic blue dress with glorious, puffy sleeves was hard to miss.

Lost Our Wonder

Maybe you continually wrestle with a sense of being an outsider too. The advent of social media does us no favors as we see in real time all the things people are doing without us. We see the promenades of couples and "tribes" walking through life in picture perfect glory. We can even sit in a crowd or at a restaurant and feel lonely and less than.

The root of our sense of insecurity is where we choose to look. We scroll through feeds and behold the images that set a bar for what we want to become. We've lost our sense of wonder for the gospel story of Jesus because we have neglected to fix our eyes on the miracle of it due to our many distractions.

When was the last time you paused to take in the brilliant colors of purple and pink in a sunset splashed through with golden sunlight and felt a sense of wonder about the One who painted that in the sky to point us to him? He is, after all, the King of the universe who displays his glory all throughout the earth, all the time.

As we turn up the volume on so many other things in our lives, we miss the gentle whispers of our God.

We miss the story that is being told every day. We miss the songs of nature that are pointing us toward him continually. While our heads are buried in screens, our eyes are diverted from the grander truth. While our ears are distracted with earbuds and the constant streaming of music and video, we miss the tiny revelations of God.

And within all this noise, within our busy lives and frantic pace, we become consumed with the question of our identity and worth. We obsessively refresh our feeds to see proof of our value through the number of likes and follows and retweets. We bombard our senses with the opinions of other people. With every glance and every thought of self, we are ever building an altar where we bow in worship to ourselves.

It destroys any sense of wonder for the very One who made us.

It escalates and elevates our sense of self by creating a pedestal of "me." Surely our identity and life purpose are all about me, right? We answer this question based on what other people say or think about us or based on our talents or activities.

The reality is that until we remove ourselves from the equation in the discovery of wholeness, we will be tossed about continually by the latest opinion from others or our latest accomplishment or failure.

Regaining a Proper Perspective of Self

In every story of the Old Testament, we see foreshadowing of the coming Messiah. The story of David and Goliath points to the perfect David who slew the giant of sin and death once and for all. The account of Noah paints a picture of the perfect Noah, the One in whom we find rescue from the deadly consequence of sin.

Within Esther 1, we find a proper perspective of self that supplies a starting point toward building a life centered on the marvelous gospel. In verse 15, King Ahasuerus consulted the wise men about what to do with Queen Vashti's disobedience according to the law. The experts had a ready answer for dealing with this queen who dared to ignore the king's orders.

Banishment.

Based on Vashti's performance, she was to be banished. When it came to judge her actions according to the law, she was to be stripped of both her position and her access to the king's presence. She was to lose these privileges due to her defiance.

For by works of the law no human being

will be justified in his sight,

since through the law

comes knowledge of sin.

Romans 3:20

Do you truly grasp your condemnation according to the law? Or do you tend to go through life feeling like a pretty good person, dismissing the pastor's sermons about repentance as mostly inapplicable to your life? We are so easily stuck in the cycle of performance, seeking to earn our way to God's favor while living and dying by the opinions of others. Simultaneously, our self-righteousness lies to us about the disturbing reality of our own wretched and sinful state.

Although Christ Jesus removed the shackles of the law, we somehow remain stuck. Our prisons are often guarded by the tenacious captor of pride. We swing violently from feeling like a failure about our performance to feeling smug about our perceived goodness.

We cannot posture our hearts in surrender, freed from the idol of self, until we stop stealing the glory from the only One worthy of it. When we choose to fall prostrate, in a regular and continual rhythm of worship, we can rightfully order our reverence for the extravagance of a grace on which we can ceaselessly feast. We can only relish the wonder of the cross when our honest and authentic heart's cry is to understand the wretch of a sinner we are, aware that we deserve banishment from the King.

Building God-Esteem

The answer to freedom is not found in any question about us at all. The greatest and most freeing discovery in our own identity is to abandon it to focus on the better question of who God is, what we think about him, and what we believe about him. To be completely freed from insecurity, we must surrender thoughts of self-esteem. Instead, we must throw the weight of these efforts toward building a healthy God-esteem.

When we begin to believe the truest realities of who God is, we become freed from ourselves. We can see ourselves not through the lens of self but rather from our identity shaped through Jesus. We become equipped to smash the idol of worshipping "me," and we can set our eyes firmly on the glory and majesty of God.

How do we grow a sense of wonder for God that will renovate our lives to grow in devotion for him and to feel his delight in us?

Thinking About God

• *When you think about God, to whom do you compare him?*

For the entirety of our lives, we fight the habit of comparing God to someone we know. We place God in the little boxes of what we have experienced in relationships with others. We are also tempted to blame God for the hard things in life. Understanding that he is a God of great love and goodness can be hard to believe when what we experience isn't good.

The Lord is compassionate and gracious, slow to anger,

abounding in love.

Psalm 103:8 (NIV)

Who has measured the waters in the hallow of his hand,

or with the breadth of his hand marked off the heavens?

Who has held the dust of the earth in a basket,

or weighed the mountains on the scales

and the hills in a balance?

Who can fathom the Spirit of the Lord,

or instruct the Lord as his counselor?

Whom did the Lord consult to enlighten him,

and who taught him the right way?

Who was it that taught him knowledge,

and showed him the path of understanding?

Isaiah 40:12-14 (NIV)

Our feelings and experiences like to be the boss. What we can feel, touch, and perceive tend to shape our opinions and thoughts about God. But the problem with letting our feelings rule is that our feelings are fleeting and ever-changing. The prophet Jeremiah warns us that our hearts are deceitful above all things (Jeremiah 17:9), and this truth tells us that listening to ourselves is a dangerous pursuit.

As long as we let our hearts direct our actions and lives, we will be tossed about on the winds of circumstance. The enduring truths of our unchanging God are found in his eternal Word. The more we dig into the Word and tether ourselves to its truths, the more rooted we become to weather any storm. This is why we continually preach the truth of God to ourselves, as found within his Word, from Genesis through Esther to Revelation. We quit listening to ourselves, and, instead, we start speaking the truth to ourselves.

48

David, whom the Bible calls a man after God's own heart, exemplifies this idea of preaching truth to our souls. The book of Psalms is full of his emotive expressions, from sadness to anger to frustration. As David cries to God honestly, we see over and again that in hard times, David learned the habit of turning his mind and thoughts to the truth of God and rehearsing them to himself.

For I hear the whispering of many—

terror on every side—

as they scheme together against me,

as they plot to take my life.

But I trust in you, O Lord;

I say, "You are my God."

My times are in your hand.

Psalm 31: 13-15a

The heavens declare the glory of God;

the skies proclaim the work of his hands.

Day after day they pour forth speech;

night after night they reveal knowledge.

They have no speech; they use no words;

no sound is heard from them.

Yet their voice goes out into all the earth,

their words to the ends of the world.

Psalm 19:1-4

• *How well are you training yourself to notice all the tiny ways that God is revealing his splendor and glory and majesty throughout every day?*

• *What are you doing, or what could you do, every day to preach truth to yourself? Do you note the truths about God seen in his Word and your life so that you can repeat them to yourself continually?*

50

It is fulfilling to our souls to think about and look for God rather than obsess about ourselves. Our deepest satisfaction can be found in realizing that, although God is unseen, his fingerprints appear all throughout our lives—we just need to look for them. When we refuse to focus our gaze on ourselves because we are too busy looking to our Father, we find a wholeness we've never known. We begin to understand who we are when we discover who God is.

Invited to Grace

Esther 1 says that Ahasuerus was a king whose splendor and glory of his majesty were ever on display and that he held a banquet for all the people, from the least to the greatest. This passage alludes to a glorious picture of God's invitation to mankind, from the least to the greatest, to come into his presence. Have you ever stopped and considered how miraculous this is for you to be included?

• *Will you take a minute, close your eyes, and whisper a prayer asking God to help you see the wonder of this invitation every day with a fresh perspective? That he who spoke the universe into existence invites YOU daily to get to know him and build a*

relationship?

God is a holy God whose presence we cannot enter as sinners such as we are. After all, the law demands we be banished due to our continual defiance. Like the commoners in Susa who were invited into the exquisite palace gardens to banquet with King Ahasuerus, we are the most unlikely guests in the kingdom of God.

Despite this astonishing invitation, we're prone to choose our own pursuits and distractions, wandering away from his presence as if the invitation were inconsequential. We disregard the sanctity and honor of coming into the presence of the King of Creation because we are just too busy to take such pauses. The familiarity of our Christianity has left a contempt for such sacred practices. We choose to fill our appetites for meaning with the empty calories of the world instead of feasting on his eternal grace.

The imagery of King Ahasuerus' seven-day banquet paints a picture of what the Bible calls our justification. The same God who displays his splendor and greatness and majesty from marvelous sunrises to star-studded nights is the very one who loves us enough to justify us, or pay the price, so that we can indeed have a place at his table.

From the beginning of the Bible to the end, we discover a continuous thread that repeats the story of God sending his Son, Jesus, to die on the cross and rise from the grave so that we can be forgiven of all sin, enjoying eternal life with him. This is the summation of the gospel.

Ahasuerus' banquet for the people of Susa, from the least to the greatest, points toward a banquet described in Luke 14:15-24. Jesus says, "Blessed is the man who will eat at the feast in the kingdom of God" (vs. 15, NIV). He goes on to tell about a man who invites honored guests to a great banquet. Many people make excuses and don't come. They are too busy pursuing their own desires and goals to accept the invitation. When the servant tells the owner of the house that the invitation is being declined, the man instructs him to "go out quickly into the streets and alleys of the town and bring in the poor, the crippled, the blind and the lame" (vs. 21).

God made a way, through Jesus, so that all can be invited to banquet with him, from the least to the greatest, in his kingdom. It was a shocking new teaching in Jesus' day to tell the exclusive religious leaders that even the lame and the poor and the crippled and blind would be able to enter the holy presence of God.

Jesus was explaining that, through his own death and resurrection, direct access to God would become available for all people, rather than just the select priests who were allowed to enter God's presence within the temple's innermost section.

For God so loved the world that he gave his only Son, that whoever believes in him should not perish but have eternal life.

John 3:16

When Jesus was brought before Pilate in Luke 23, Pilate asked the Jewish people who demanded Jesus' death, "Why? What evil has he done? I have found in him no guilt deserving death. I will therefore punish and release him (vs. 22)." Jesus was the only one ever on earth, in all of history, who could stand before God and have it said, "there is no guilt in him deserving death." Yet, he surrendered himself to death for everyone on earth, in all of history, who did deserve death so that his righteousness could cover us.

Let me say that again. The Almighty God willed that his beloved Son would be forsaken by him on the cross, so that we, who have no right to the King, can be made heirs and sons of God.

Yet we dare to skip through our days letting our own agenda and the approval of others sit on the throne of our hearts. Why do we allow such wanderings from true fulfillment?

Jesus chose obedience again and again out of his love for his Father. He endured all that his life included because his eyes were fixed squarely on his Father's will. Do we do the same? Are we growing in affinity for our Father?

We are loved with an unfailing love, yet we pour ourselves out for lesser things. Most days we don't even think about the miracle of this banquet invitation. We've lost our sense of astonishment that God the Father allowed his Son to be the sacrificial Lamb so that the feast of grace could happen in the first place.

Choosing the Cup

In ancient Jewish tradition, a young couple sealed their marriage covenant during a betrothal ceremony by sharing a cup of wine.[1] The groom would offer it to the bride, and she would take it to drink as a symbol of her decision to enter the covenant. We, too, as the bride of Christ, were offered a symbolic cup of wine by the Bridegroom as pictured through the Last Supper.

Even as Christ prayed in distress to the point of sweating blood in the Garden of Gethsemane, he asked the Father if the cup might pass from him. Then, moments before his arrest, Jesus declared that he would drink the bitter cup of crucifixion, having his own blood spilled, because it was the Father's will. Through the sacrament of communion, we are to remind ourselves of the invitation to dine with the triune God, of the cost that was paid for us, and of our ongoing decision to honor our covenant relationship as believers in Jesus. In Esther 1:7-8, the royal wine flowed freely, and it was "lavished according to the bounty of the king" (v. 7b). Do you see it? King Ahasuerus, motivated by pride, threw an elaborate and expensive feast with free-flowing wine in order to show off his splendor.

But God.

God, motivated by love, throws an extravagant and costly feast. With the blood of his own Son flowing freely, according to the bounty of his grace, He lavishes his love on us so that we can be called the children of God (1 John 3:1).

We have a decision to make. The decision is all ours, and nobody else can make it for us. A look at the compound Hebrew root words describing the free-flowing wine from Ahasuerus' feast informs us that each one was to drink as much as he wanted, with no one compelling him to do so, as it was his own choice to make. ₂

All we have to do is join the meal, accept the cup as the ancient Jewish brides did, and choose to banquet with the Father, rather than the world, seeking to keep a wide-eyed wonder at the invitation.

While they were eating, Jesus took bread, gave thanks and broke it, and gave it to his disciples, saying, "Take and eat; this is my body." Then he took the cup, gave thanks and offered it to them, saying, "Drink from it, all of you. This is the blood of my covenant, which is poured out for many for the forgiveness of sins."

Matthew 26: 26-28 (NIV)

Response to Esther 1

The Word of God is meant to transform and call us to action. Take some time to consider the questions below and write out your responses.

• *Have you come to the banquet of grace? Have you accepted God's invitation to dwell in his presence and drink from the cup that was spilled for you?*

• *Do you continually partake in this feast of grace? Do you routinely take time to thank him and quiet your heart with the truth of his forgiveness and release from the banishment that the law demands for your performance?*

• *Does your life regularly tell others around you about the King who offers a banquet of grace? Does your life reflect the bitter cup of obedience that Jesus himself took for us, responding with your own obedience to the Father, even when it's hard?*

• *How often are you feasting in God's presence? How are you intentionally trying to listen tom seek, and worship God? Do you see this as a privilege, and do you grasp how you deserve to be banished from his presence?*

The Truths of Esther 1

Let's wrap up this section of Scripture by considering these three elements.

1—Adoration of God from Esther 1

- You are the God of all splendor.

- You are the God who invites us to your banqueting table to feast on grace.

- You are the God who is slow to anger and abounding in love.

- You are the God who is all knowing and requires no counsel from anyone.

- You are the God who freed us from the law that requires our banishment.

2—Affirmation of Our Gospel Identity from Esther 1

- I am a witness to his splendor.

- I am invited in and included to the banqueting table of the King of all creation.

- I am not banished as I deserve.

- I am secure and accepted in the love of God through Jesus.

- I am the recipient of God's covenant of love.

- I am freed from the law through God's justification.

- I am not captive by man's opinion, pride, or the law.

3—Actions to Take from Esther 1

- I am to accept God's invitation by accepting Christ's death on the cross for my sins and choosing to follow Jesus, surrendering to him more and more.

- I am to feast on the abundance that God provides.

- I am to look for his splendor.

- I am not to operate out of anger or fear or bow to man's approval.

- I am to seek God's counsel daily through prayer and the Word of God.

- I am to come to the table of grace daily and be ever in awe that I am able to do so.

Conclusion of Esther 1

Esther 1 points to the gospel story. According to the law, we should be banished from God's presence. But the powerful, majestic God of splendor and glory invites us to his banquet because he chose to allow his Son to become the Lamb of God who was sacrificed for our sins. We are called to live in awe that the powerful King of the universe would dare to let us not only see his glorious kingdom but invite us to have a part in his kingdom's story.

When we start to lose our wonder about this—when life's hardships and battles and distractions become all that we can see—we must remember to turn our gaze to Jesus. We must build the habit of looking long into the Word of God, thinking on his love, and preaching his truths to ourselves. Let love stir within us for the King who loves us extravagantly and invites us to dine with him. May we never get over that invitation.

ESTHER 2

Now when the turn came for each young woman to go to King Ahasuerus, after being twelve months under the regulations for the women, since this was the regular period of their beautifying....

Esther 2:12

[He] set the royal crown upon her head and made her queen instead of Vashti.

Esther 2:17b

And it was recorded in the book of the chronicles in the presence of the king.

Esther 2:23b

Esther 2, *English Standard Version*

Esther Chosen Queen

2 After these things, when the anger of King Ahasuerus had abated, he remembered Vashti and what she had done and what had been decreed against her. 2 Then the king's young men who attended him said, "Let beautiful young virgins be sought out for the king. 3 And let the king appoint officers in all the provinces of his kingdom to gather all the beautiful young virgins to the harem in Susa the citadel, under custody of Hegai, the king's eunuch, who is in charge of the women. Let their cosmetics be given them. 4 And let the young woman who pleases the king be queen instead of Vashti." This pleased the king, and he did so.

5 Now there was a Jew in Susa the citadel whose name was Mordecai, the son of Jair, son of Shimei, son of Kish, a Benjaminite, 6 who had been carried away from Jerusalem among the captives carried away with Jeconiah king of Judah, whom Nebuchadnezzar king of Babylon had carried away. 7 He was bringing up Hadassah, that is Esther, the daughter of his uncle, for she had neither father nor mother. The young woman had a beautiful

figure and was lovely to look at, and when her father and her mother died, Mordecai took her as his own daughter. 8 So when the king's order and his edict were proclaimed, and when many young women were gathered in Susa the citadel in custody of Hegai, Esther also was taken into the king's palace and put in custody of Hegai, who had charge of the women. 9 And the young woman pleased him and won his favor. And he quickly provided her with her cosmetics and her portion of food, and with seven chosen young women from the king's palace and advanced her and her young women to the best place in the harem. 10 Esther had not made known her people or kindred, for Mordecai had commanded her not to make it known. 11 And every day Mordecai walked in front of the court of the harem to learn how Esther was and what was happening to her.

12 Now when the turn came for each young woman to go in to King Ahasuerus, after being twelve months under the regulations for the women, since this was the regular period of their beautifying, six months with oil of myrrh and six months with spices and ointments for women— 13 when the young woman went in to the king in this way, she was given whatever she desired to take with her from the

harem to the king's palace. 14 In the evening she would go in, and in the morning, she would return to the second harem in custody of Shaashgaz, the king's eunuch, who was in charge of the concubines. She would not go in to the king again, unless the king delighted in her and she was summoned by name.

15 When the turn came for Esther the daughter of Abihail the uncle of Mordecai, who had taken her as his own daughter, to go in to the king, she asked for nothing except what Hegai the king's eunuch, who had charge of the women, advised. Now Esther was winning favor in the eyes of all who saw her. 16 And when Esther was taken to King Ahasuerus, into his royal palace, in the tenth month, which is the month of Tebeth, in the seventh year of his reign, 17 the king loved Esther more than all the women, and she won grace and favor in his sight more than all the virgins, so that he set the royal crown on her head and made her queen instead of Vashti. 18 Then the king gave a great feast for all his officials and servants; it was Esther's feast. He also granted a remission of taxes to the provinces and gave gifts with royal generosity.

Mordecai Discovers a Plot

19 Now when the virgins were gathered together the second time, Mordecai was sitting at the king's gate. 20 Esther had not made known her kindred or her people, as Mordecai had commanded her, for Esther obeyed Mordecai just as when she was brought up by him. 21 In those days, as Mordecai was sitting at the king's gate, Bigthan and Teresh, two of the king's eunuchs, who guarded the threshold, became angry and sought to lay hands on King Ahasuerus. 22 And this came to the knowledge of Mordecai, and he told it to Queen Esther, and Esther told the king in the name of Mordecai. 23 When the affair was investigated and found to be so, the men were both hanged on the gallows. And it was recorded in the book of the chronicles in the presence of the king.

THE NOW AND THE YET TO COME

Esther 2

I am a goal-oriented, Type A, recovering perfectionist. Yes, as a matter of fact, I add something to a task list that I've already done so that I can check it off. Since college, I have lived and died by my paper planner, adding all manner of tasks and then gleefully highlighting them in yellow once they are accomplished.

From the time I was little, my worth has been tied to my performance. My day could be ruined by a teacher's corrections written in red, while a good grade brought great satisfaction. A high score WITH a scratch and sniff sticker on the paper? Well, this was the pinnacle of my early childhood, since I spent hours cataloging my sticker collection into a photo album with separate sections for puffy stickers, Holly Hobby stickers, and the coveted scratch and sniff variety.

I distinctly remember a particular sticker that my grandparents sent after their trip to Australia. The round sticker featured a patchwork lion with these words printed around the edges: "Please be patient. God isn't through with me yet." I felt both encouraged and judged at the same time. Were they speaking to my flaws, letting me know that they saw them as much as I did? Or were they reassuring me that it was okay to have flaws? Oh, the conflict I felt. I knew then that while I relish results, I needed to embrace that life is full of ongoing processes.

Looking Ahead, Not Behind

As the sand in the hourglass falls exponentially faster toward the launch of my children from home, I find the questions multiplying within my mother's heart. Did I teach them all the things that needed to be taught along the way? Did I do well by this sacred mission of motherhood? How do I release my supervision of this child whom I taught to eat with a spoon?

I know I'm not alone in this internal debate, but I came into motherhood with some baggage. There were deep wounds and losses, which, left to their own devices, filled me with doubt and rejection. Eventually, with biblical counseling and tearful prayers, I came to a freeing epiphany. I'll save you some money in therapy and share it.

We cannot change our heritage, but we can change our legacy.

This, in fact, is the miracle of what God does for us through the gospel.

All of your past history, in the hands of the Redeemer, becomes beauty from ashes. Rather than holding you captive, your wounds can become a catalyst for new things once they're surrendered to the heavenly Father.

They shall build up the ancient ruins;

they shall raise up the former devastations;

they shall repair the ruined cities,

the devastations of many generations.

Isaiah 61:4

Freedom is found in taking the pain and energy from rehearsing old baggage and using them instead to rebuild ancient ruins, rise up out of former devastations, and change the legacy from the destruction of many generations.

We see this truth so clearly in the life of Esther here in chapter 2. Esther was a female orphaned captive, living in exile in the citadel of Susa. She was a Jewess of the tribe of Benjamin, and, lest we forget, Benjamin was the youngest of Jacob's sons and last in line for inheritance rights. Esther's past seemed to dictate a dim future. According to her history and status, Esther couldn't have imagined God's purposes or processes for her. She was just a young girl, approximately fourteen years of age, who was raised by her cousin after her parent's death. Esther's radical transformation through divine providence points to this biblical truth.

He raises up the poor from the dust;

he lifts the needy from the ash heap

to make them sit with princes

and inherit a seat of honor.

For the pillars of the earth are the LORD's,

and on them he has set the world.

1 Samuel 2:8

When we set our eyes on our losses, we become blind to the purpose God can bring. When we focus on the wounds from others more than the wounds of Jesus, we become paralyzed.

The writer of Esther is clear about her lowly position as one least likely to rise to a notable position. She was the most implausible candidate for queen, much less the invitation for inclusion in divine plans to preserve the nation of Israel.

The Father to the fatherless loves to use the most inconceivable people to accomplish his eternal purposes. Against the backdrop of our greatest weaknesses, his unfathomable strength is undeniable. You are never counted out in the economy of God, so don't excuse yourself from the race. Keep praying. Keep seeking. Keep asking. Keep telling the Lord that you are willing for your pain to be used for his purposes. Allow him to use your scars for those with open wounds.

Embracing the Process

I was sitting in a crowded sanctuary at the Proclaim Conference when the speaker's words hit my heart as if I were the only person in the room. Lauren Chandler said that God loves us too much to not continually transform us to reflect him in increasing measure; he loves us too much to leave us as we are. Through her teaching, I saw a new hopeful purpose within life's painful trials.

Esther 2:3 gives a picture of this biblical process also known as sanctification. The king ordered all the beautiful young women in the citadel of Susa to be gathered to the palace under the custody of his eunuch, Hegai. The women then underwent a required twelve-month beautification process before they could enter the king's presence.

Having exceptional natural beauty wasn't enough. They needed to be beautified more. Likewise, though the cross justifies us, our lives should be marked by the process of being sanctified, or transformed, as we grow in understanding and knowledge of the King of Creation. Often, our most dramatic transformations are born from seasons of hardship.

Examining the Sanctification Process

When looking at the ancient Persian beauty rituals through the lens of Scripture, we find instruction for our sanctification process. John Wesley's explanatory commentary on Esther 2 describes the beautification rituals as a time for "purification, when the women were to be cleansed from impurities to perfume, adorn, and prepare for the king." [1]

Isn't our earthly life a precursor and preparation for an eternity with our King, living in his presence? Let's consider some of the ancient beauty rituals to find clarity for our ongoing process of reflecting Christ in increasing measure.

• **Incense**—Part of the Persian year-long treatment that the girls in the palace received included myrrh, which is an incense and aroma. Scripture uses both incense and aroma as symbols to describe our prayers, actions, and offerings. These biblical examples show spiritual disciplines that work to transform us toward reflecting God.

May my prayer be set before you like incense;

may the lifting up of my hands be like the evening sacrifices.

Psalm 141:2 (NIV)

I have received full payment and even more,

I am amply supplied, now that I have received from Epaphroditus

the gifts you sent. They are a fragrant offering, an acceptable

sacrifice, pleasing to God.

Philippians 4:18 (NIV)

And when he had taken it, the four living creatures and the twenty-

four elders fell down before the Lamb. Each one had a harp and

they were holding golden bowls full of incense, which are the

prayers of the saints.

Revelations 5:8 (NIV)

⸻

• **Cleansings**—The women at the palace went through ritual

cleansings as part of their beauty regiment, plucking eyebrows and

removing body hair through waxing. The most fundamental

component of sanctification is the cutting away of our fleshly

desires, mirroring the work of the cross where Jesus offered up his

flesh in obedience to the will of the Father. Throughout both the Old

and New Testament, we find references to how the Jewish practice of

circumcision exemplifies the idea of circumcising our hearts to cut

away what needs to be cleared.

As we pursue living as Jesus followers, we are to be evaluating the habits and idols that need to be removed to make room for God. Replacing worthless idols and sinful obstacles with rightful thinking about God is paramount to reflecting him more. Intentionally and continually agreeing with God about our sin through confession is fundamental to our transformation.

Therefore, since we are surrounded by such a great cloud of witnesses, let us throw off everything that hinders and the sin that so easily entangles. And let us run with perseverance the race marked out for us.

Hebrews 12:1 (NIV)

If we confess our sins, he is faithful and just and will forgive us our sins and purify us from all unrighteousness.

1 John 1:9 (NIV)

• **Henna paintings**—Ancient Persian brides, such as Ahasuerus' queen candidates, painted their hands and feet with henna to mark themselves as belonging to their groom. Within the radical gospel story, Jesus, the bridegroom, flips the script by marking himself for each of us. We, the bride of Christ, are distinguished as belonging to God the Father because of the nail-scarred hands and feet of Jesus. Jesus' death abolished any need for the rituals of continual animal sacrifices to earn the status of forgiveness and belonging.

> *But he was pierced for our transgressions;*
>
> *he was crushed for our iniquities;*
>
> *upon him was the chastisement*
>
> *that brought us peace,*
>
> *and with his wounds we are healed.*
>
> *Isaiah 53:5 (NIV)*

• **Clothing**—Each of the queen candidates was allowed to choose anything she desired from the harem's palace to take to the king's palace. However, even the most lavish robes in the palace of King Ahasuerus cannot compare to what Scripture says about our wardrobe. Look at how Isaiah describes even our best efforts to live a righteous life or to become worthy by our own striving.

All of us have become like one who is unclean,

and all our righteous acts are like filthy rags;

we all shrivel up like a leaf, and like the wind our sins sweep us

away. Isaiah 64:6 (NIV)

Again, the cross accomplished for us what we could not do on our own, for our finest efforts on our best day are but filthy rags. Following Jesus in ongoing surrender means that we are issued new garments, wrapped in the righteousness he offers.

I delight greatly in the Lord, my soul rejoices in my God.

For he has clothed me with garments of salvation

and arrayed me in a robe of righteousness,

as a bridegroom adorns his head like a priest,

and as a bride adorns herself with jewels.

Isaiah 61:10 (NIV)

Though the queen candidates entered King Ahasuerus' presence having been primped and made over, God does the work himself to beautify us through the death and resurrection of the Son and the continual work of the Holy Spirit within us. God is transforming us every day as we surrender to him to do so. Sanctification is the work of the triune God in our hearts and minds.

Working Out Our Sanctification

The word "beautify" as seen in ancient texts can be defined as "to glorify, or to honor with admiration." 2 Like these women in Susa, we are created with an innate desire for admiration. Left to our own devices, we seek this for ourselves, craving the applause of others in order to be seen and celebrated.

Yet our natural desire for self-exaltation clashes with God's holiness. On the battleground of yielding self-focused accolades to the glory of God alone, we learn to avoid stealing the praise from the only deserving One. This is the work of sanctification—being transformed from selfish desires to obedience for the sake of God's name only.

In the same way, let your light shine before others, that they may see your good deeds and glorify your Father in heaven.

Matthew 5:16 (NIV)

Using our moments on Earth to point others to the splendor of God is the most beautiful way to live a life of eternal significance. Fixing our eyes to the kingdom to come beckons us to pursue God's glory with every day of our lives, throwing our time, talents, and energies toward this objective.

Becoming Radiant

In pursuing transformation, Scripture explains that we are radiant when we reflect God's glory in our lives. We can tend to overcomplicate the idea of obedience to God by imagining that we must surrender to full-time ministry or perform huge demonstrative acts of self-denial in order to best reflect God's glory.

Yet, in Exodus 34, Moses is described as radiant, or reflecting God, after he simply spent time with him. In fact, Moses' time with the Lord made his face glow to the point of requiring a veil to avoid blinding other people.

And we, who with unveiled faces all reflect the Lord's glory, are being transformed into his likeness with ever increasing glory, which comes from the Lord, who is the Spirit.

2 Corinthians 3:18

If you want to know how to press into the process of sanctification, make it a daily habit to spend time with God. Sanctification occurs as we read his Word and pray—through speaking and listening. One of the most useful tools that I've found to this end is writing out my prayers and reflections from Bible reading to keep me focused and engaged.

Sanctification also happens during regular rhythms of corporate worship in a local church and when gathering with other believers. It happens through actively serving other people and having conversations focused on speaking truth and grace. It's intentionally investing time to know God more, which naturally stimulates increasing love for him. The result of these spiritual practices is reflecting God more by being transformed through a growing intimacy with him. This is sanctification, beauty, and radiance.

How Sanctifications Impacts Relationships

As we nurture a wonder toward our justification and embrace the process of sanctification, we gain freedom while building confidence in God's grace. Centering our focus on our own transformation is a key to overcoming comparison, as it rightly sets our hearts to look up rather than around and it keeps our own process as our focal point.

Furthermore, shifting our interactions so that we care more about how God is perceived than how we are noticed will equip us to endure jealousy, gossip, and loneliness. This rightful centering of our heart for the Lord brings order to relationships with others.

When we preach to our souls that our heavenly Father loves us too much to let us stay how we are, then we are free to float in the grace of God and to extend that grace to others. As we gain knowledge and belief in God's unfailing love toward us, we become equipped to live out God's call of radical generosity. Understanding the depth of God's grace to save *and* transform us, we are able to live a life filled with compassion toward the lowly, the unkind, and the difficult people around us.

Looking Past Our Sanctification: The Yet to Come

As I've grown in my faith, I've become confident that there's nothing on this earth that I'll miss when I'm brought into the presence of my Heavenly Father. That is what we are all actually made for—to finally be completed and perfected in the presence of God. Eternity was set in the hearts of all men (Ecclesiastes 3:11), and it is where all want will unimaginably be erased, and absolute fulfillment will be enjoyed.

The older I get, the more I long for this ultimate reality and the more real it becomes to me. This is partly due to considering my mortality as I get older. But the greater reason that eternity has become more real is because I've felt the slightest touch of it. While sitting with loved ones passing from Earth to their anticipated home in heaven, I've had the most profound, indescribable feeling as though the veil between heaven and Earth had thinned to the point that a palpable sensation caused my heart to stir and my skin to tingle.

Most recently, I stayed overnight in hospice with my husband's grandmother. I knew that, despite some obstacles, I needed to get to Houston to take that Tuesday night shift. I felt certain it was my task to sit with her that night, although, in truth, it was a sacred privilege. Never in my life have I experienced something so sweet and precious as being in that room when the divine reached in and touched Earth as 95-year-old Mamaw was welcomed into the arms of the Savior she served so well.

That's how I know that heaven is real and that's why I long for it more and more.

Here on this earth, we are strangers and aliens, much like Esther was as a Jew living in Susa. We can find endurance through life knowing there's a day coming when we're promised a never-ending "happily ever after," enjoying our citizenship in heaven.

First, God justified us through Jesus. Then, he sanctifies us through the Holy Spirit. What's coming next is our glorification where we will be made completely whole as we enter the presence of the King of the universe.

He set the royal crown on her head and made her queen instead of Vashti. And the king gave a great banquet, Esther's banquet, for all his nobles and officials. He proclaimed a holiday throughout the province and distributed gifts with royal liberality.

Esther 2:17b – 18 (NIV)

Esther was an orphaned foreigner brought into the palace to go through the preparation process for meeting the king in person. In Esther's banquet, the king gave Esther a crown, and she takes a new role within the kingdom as she was welcomed fully in the presence of the king.

This scene from Esther's wedding feast alludes to other celebrations found within Scripture.

So, he [the prodigal son] got up and went to his father.

But while he was still a long way off, his father saw him and was

filled with compassion for him; he ran to his son, threw his arms

around him and kissed him. The son said to him, "Father, I have

sinned against heaven and against you. I am no longer worthy to

be called your son." But the Father said to his servants, "Quick!

Bring the best robe and put it on him. Put a ring on his finger and

sandals on his feet.

Bring the fattened calf and kill it. Let's have a feast and celebrate.

For this son of mine was dead and is alive again; he

was lost and is found." So, they began to celebrate.

Luke 15:20-24 (NIV)

Do not let your hearts be troubled. You believe in God; believe also

in me. My father's house has many rooms; if that were not so,

would I have told you that I am going there to prepare a place for

you? And if I go and prepare a place for you, I will come back and take you to be with me that you also may be where I am. You know

the way to the place where I am going.

John 14:1-4 (NIV)

Then I heard what sounded like a great multitude, like the roar of

the rushing waters and like the loud peals of thunder, shouting,

"Hallelujah! For our Lord God Almighty reigns. Let us rejoice and

be glad and give him glory! For the wedding of the Lamb has

come, and his bride has made herself ready. Fine linen, bright and

clean, was given her to wear." (Fine linen stands for the righteous

acts of God's holy people). Then the angel said to me, "Write this:

Blessed are those who are invited to the wedding supper of the

Lamb!" And he added, "These are the true words of God."

Revelations 19:6-9 (NIV)

We see ourselves in Esther's story and in the story of the prodigal son who at last comes home and is greeted with a celebration by his father.

Jesus promised his disciples just before his death that he is preparing a home for us in eternity, and he will return to Earth to rule and reign forevermore. This is the unending celebration to come.

As foretold in Revelation, there will be a great wedding supper of the Lamb of God within the eternal kingdom. We will have a seat at the table.

We have been justified. We are being sanctified. We will be glorified for all of eternity as we are made whole and perfect in the presence of our King, living in a kingdom with no more tears, death, or darkness.

Heaven is coming. What we see and experience here on Earth feels so real, but our ultimate reality is the unseen and foggy kingdom to come. In that coming kingdom, we, the sons and daughters of God, will reign as co-heirs alongside Jesus in the new heavens and the new Earth.

We can live within our broken world, with all its troubles, by setting our eyes on the celebration to come when we are welcomed by the Father. All that is wrong will be made right.

Pressing on Until Then

The second chapter of Esther closes with what feels like a random narrative recounting a thwarted assassination plot against King Ahasuerus. Mordecai himself, there at the king's gate, overheard two of the king's officials from the king's inner circle. For unknown reasons, they were enraged to the point of taking Ahasuerus' life. Mordecai, serving loyally as a porter or doorkeeper of the courts, overheard and reported the situation to Esther.

These actions highlight a remarkable characteristic about Mordecai, which is his faithfulness in the mundane. He was just going about his day, doing his work and dutifully overseeing Esther's well-being as best as he could from the palace gates when he found himself perfectly positioned to hear the conversation of these two eunuchs, Bigthan and Teresh.

Mordecai had a choice to make. Would he use this information to protect the king or just keep going about his day?

I often ponder the unspoken details from Scripture, such as the thought process of Mordecai in this moment. It would stand to reason that Mordecai wasn't fond of Ahasuerus. After all, his beloved cousin was taken away and had been kept from him at a distance for over a year. What we know of Ahasuerus isn't particularly flattering, as he was one who drank too much, acted rashly, and relied on the advice of others for important decisions. It would seem that no one would ever know if Mordecai chose to stay silent. Silence would have also protected him from becoming a target to these powerful nobles or their allies.

Yet Mordecai chose to act bravely. In an ordinary day, doing regular things, Mordecai made a big choice with no guarantee of the outcome. We know from the end of Esther 2 that Mordecai successfully saved the king from the plot and the would-be assassins were hung, as was recorded in the king's book of annals.

For Mordecai, there's no reward or promotion. There's no immediate gratification or even acknowledgment of the risk he took. The event was written down, and he went on about his life doing his regular thing. Nothing changed for Mordecai. At least at this point.

All that happened for Mordecai was that the details were recorded in the "book of the chronicles in the presence of the king" (Esther 2:32).

Your eyes saw my unformed substance;
in your book were written, every one of them,
the days that were formed for me,

when as yet there was none of them.

Psalm 139:16

If you ever doubt that your ordinary tedious days between now and heaven matter in the scope of eternity, I assure you that they do. The same exact language used in Esther 2:32 is used again in Psalm 139:16 to describe a book of days written in the presence of the King.

Your days matter. He is the God who sees. You may not see any result from your actions or from your daily wrestling to pursue God. You may not know if anyone noticed or if any transformation is happening through the daily and incremental efforts to serve him, but the King takes notice. The King, who is not bound by time or anything else, sees. He knows every day already. Your future is history to him, and he sees every single detail.

Your tedious offerings in your daily grind are not hidden. They are written in the book of days by the Ancient of Days. Forevermore.

Response to Esther 2

The Word of God is meant to transform and call us to action. Take some time to consider the questions below and write out your responses.

• *What is in your past history – wounds, losses, or failures – that tends to crowd your thoughts and keep a hold on you? What are the "ruins" chaining you down?*

• *If these are significant enough to affect your ability to function daily, have you ever considered biblical counseling or letting someone know you might need help?*

• *How could God use these things for his purposes? What legacy could come from your history—what beauty from these ashes? How might God transform you through your pain and also bring new purpose for others?*

• *What are you doing daily to lean into the process of becoming more like Jesus? What are your regular habits that encourage sanctification?*

• *Are you confident of God's grace over you? Do you feel God's delight and favor? If you don't regularly feel his delight, begin to pray that he will help you do so.*

• *Who is a "least" in your midst that you can befriend, following the example of Esther, who built rapport with the eunuch overseeing her? Who do you see regularly, such as the coffee shop barista or store clerk, and how might you seek to build a relationship with them to show them that they matter to you – and ultimately, to God?*

• *What about your life feels so mundane and ordinary that you can't fathom how it can be used for the eternal kingdom?*

• Picture the day you come into the face-to-face presence of the Almighty God. Consider journaling about how you picture it. Sit and think on this to be encouraged.

The Truths of Esther 2

Let's wrap up this section of Scripture by considering these three elements.

1—Adoration of God from Esther 2

- You are the God who changes our history for your legacy.
- You are the God who cares for our needs, as surely as Mordecai and Hegai cared for Esther's.
- You are the God who stays near us, like Mordecai who paced at the gates, staying near Esther.

- You are the God who is ever transforming us through sanctification so that we reflect you more.

- You are the God who sent his Son to die so that we are invited to the Wedding Banquet of the Lamb.

- You are the God ever watching for us, running to meet us to invite us into your house forever.

- You are the God who invites us to dine at your table, every day of our lives, where you provide the abundant feast of grace and love and renewal.

- You are the God who crowns us with eternal life, as surely as Esther was crowned as queen.

- You are the God who notes all of our days and details and uses them for your purposes.

2—Affirmation of Our Gospel Identity from Esther 2

- I am not defined by my history but by God's love.

- I am cared for by God who meets my needs and to whom I belong.

- I am no longer a slave, captive, exile, or an orphan who has no place.

- I am being sanctified and am a work in progress all throughout my life, as I obediently follow God.

- I am covered in God's grace that transforms and renews me.

- I am not defined by others around me or my circumstances, but by what the gospel says about me.

- I am given garments of salvation in exchange for the filthy rags of my sinful self.

- I am chosen and approved and have favor with God through Jesus.

- I am made radiant, reflecting God's glory as I spend time with him.

- I am crowned with eternal life and invited to God's banquet table.

- I am a citizen of heaven, where the glory will be so marvelous that it cannot compare to the troubles I endure on Earth.

3—Actions to Take from Esther 2

- I am to surrender my history to God.

- I am to come to the table of grace through Jesus, day after day.

- I am to reject any lie that steals the truthful thoughts of God or my gospel identity.

- I am to stand firmly in my identity as a sinner saved by grace and changed by God's on-going presence in my life as I obey him.

- I am to see the lowly around me and form a relationship with them, carrying forward the rhythm of the gospel.

- I am to rise above comparison and competition by fixing my eyes on the God who loves and changes me.

- I am to rest in the grace and care of God through Jesus instead of trying to earn my position in the kingdom of God.

- I am to seek daily time with God as part of my role in sanctification.

- I am to obey God and use my life to glorify him instead of stealing his glory by seeking my own.

- I am to continually be awed and humbled at the price paid to bring me to God's table.

- I am to feast on the abundance of God rather than gorge on the fleeting things of this earth.

- I am to stand firm in my identity through the gospel, with the hope of eternity.

- I am to invite others to come to the table of God.

- I am to live here on Earth with my heavenly home in mind, motivated to fight the good fight of faith on Earth and store up my treasures in heaven.

Conclusion of Esther 2

The Rhythm of a Gospel-Centered Life

Justification. Jesus' life, death, and resurrection opened our invitation to become children of God—for everyone, from the least to the greatest. May we live in wonder of this justification.

Sanctification. As we accept God's invitation into his kingdom, he is ever transforming us to his image. We are being made radiant as we are renewed through time in God's presence—through prayer and praise and reading the Bible. We beautify ourselves, not with make-up or our hair or our clothes, but by bringing honor and praise to God's name. For God alone is worthy of all attention. We are not to steal his glory by seeking our own fame. We find our purpose in bringing glory to him, even in the unseen day-to-day tasks. May we continually surrender to the process of being transformed.

Glorification. We have a banquet yet to come that will put all other banquets and celebrations to shame. We will run to see our heavenly Father face-to-face and feel his embrace as we are crowned with eternal life. May we set our eyes toward our ultimate glorification as motivation to press on.

ESTHER 3

"Why do you transgress the king's command?" Day after day they

spoke to him, but he refused to comply.

Esther 3:3b-4a

Esther 3, *English Standard Version*

Haman Plots Against the Jews

3 After these things King Ahasuerus promoted Haman the Agagite, the son of Hammedatha, and advanced him and set his throne above all the officials who were with him. ₂ And all the king's servants who were at the king's gate bowed down and paid homage to Haman, for the king had so commanded concerning him. But Mordecai did not bow down or pay homage. ₃ Then the king's servants who were at the king's gate said to Mordecai, "Why do you transgress the king's command?" ₄ And when they spoke to him day after day and he would not listen to them, they told Haman, in order to see whether Mordecai's words would stand, for he had told them that he was a Jew. ₅ And when Haman saw that Mordecai did not bow down or pay homage to him, Haman was filled with fury. ₆ But he disdained to lay hands on Mordecai alone. So, as they had made known to him the people of Mordecai, Haman sought to destroy all the Jews, the people of Mordecai, throughout the whole kingdom of Ahasuerus.

₇ In the first month, which is the month of Nisan, in the twelfth year of King Ahasuerus, they cast Pur (that is, they cast lots) before

Haman day after day; and they cast it month after month till the twelfth month, which is the month of Adar. 8 Then Haman said to King Ahasuerus, "There is a certain people scattered abroad and dispersed among the peoples in all the provinces of your kingdom. Their laws are different from those of every other people, and they do not keep the king's laws, so that it is not to the king's profit to tolerate them. 9 If it please the king, let it be decreed that they be destroyed, and I will pay 10,000 talents of silver into the hands of those who have charge of the king's business, that they may put it into the king's treasuries." 10 So the king took his signet ring from his hand and gave it to Haman the Agagite, the son of Hammedatha, the enemy of the Jews. 11 And the king said to Haman, "The money is given to you, the people also, to do with them as it seems good to you."

12 Then the king's scribes were summoned on the thirteenth day of the first month, and an edict, according to all that Haman commanded, was written to the king's satraps and to the governors over all the provinces and to the officials of all the peoples, to every province in its own script and every people in its own language. It

was written in the name of King Ahasuerus and sealed with the king's signet ring. 13 Letters were sent by couriers to all the king's provinces with instruction to destroy, to kill, and to annihilate all Jews, young and old, women and children, in one day, the thirteenth day of the twelfth month, which is the month of Adar, and to plunder their goods. 14 A copy of the document was to be issued as a decree in every province by proclamation to all the peoples to be ready for that day. 15 The couriers went out hurriedly by order of the king, and the decree was issued in Susa the citadel. And the king and Haman sat down to drink, but the city of Susa was thrown into confusion.

A FAITHFUL LIFE
Esther 3

Last spring, my daughter and I watched part of the funeral for President George H.W. Bush. His was a life well-lived and a death noted around the globe. For days, coverage of his life chronicled his remarkable military career, his astounding marriage of seventy-three years, and his many political accomplishments. He was remembered as funny and faithful, with a love for family and country, and, most of all, a steadfast love for God.

Nearly six years ago, another funeral occurred to mark another life well-lived. They were of the same generation, but, unlike the passing of the former president, no crowds lined up or filled a church to celebrate the life of Thelma Jean Cooper Anthony. Her name is not recognizable, and no fame or fortune was earned in her life.

But Mamaw's life was equally important. She was as devoted to her tasks and faith as George H.W. Bush, and in many ways even more so because she chose to press on anonymously. Mamaw grew up poor, the daughter of farmers in Krum, Texas. Her parents worked the land to provide for their children. She relished her days going to school and helped out at home as did her siblings. Since Krum didn't have its own school, she went to the nearby town of Prosper. Mamaw loved learning and was proud to say that she graduated as valedictorian of her class of sixteen pupils from Prosper High School.

Once she married, Mamaw woke up daily to fix an egg sandwich and pack a lunch for her husband before his 4:00 a.m. shift at the factory. She endured numerous miscarriages before finally giving birth to my mother-in-law, who required a risky life-or-death surgery at birth. Mamaw cared for elderly parents and in-laws in her 800-square-foot home and often took in her three nieces when their mother was hospitalized. She helped raise her grandson and babysat his cousins, and she stayed active in her church until age finally caused her to move into an assisted living facility.

Mamaw spent countless hours rocking my three babies in her lap and reading stacks of books to them. She never wanted to be a bother to anyone as she preferred being the helper. One time, she laid on her bathroom floor at the assisted living facility for thirteen hours overnight. When we arrived at the emergency room with her, she said she didn't hit her Life Alert® button because she didn't want to inconvenience anyone.

Mamaw did the simple, tedious, and mundane in her life of ninety-five years. She never dined with heads of state, and she certainly never put on or put up with pretenses. But she loved well. With all that she could bring to the table, she loved with extravagance and generosity. She showed the love of her Savior to those around her.

That's a faithful life—choosing to make the best of what life gave her, to keep on, day after day, though no one noticed, and to serve for the sake of love with no honor or fortune granted in this life. Hers is a worthy example to emulate. Like the widow woman who gave her only two coins in Mark 12:42, Mamaw contributed what she had to meet the needs of others.

We need not seek the praise of man or the fortunes of this world. We need not compare ourselves to those with large platforms and huge audiences. When we wake up every day and choose to love those in our paths and do our tasks to the best of our ability, offering up the meager loaves and fishes we possess (Matthew 14) to the hands of the Father, then we are choosing that which is most worthwhile.

Man's Empty Praise

After being promoted to "a throne above all the officials who were with him" (Esther 3:1), one would think that Haman would've been satisfied not only by his position but also by the honor others paid him. He enjoyed the applause and attention of the people as they bowed before him—with the exception of one exiled Jewish man.

The fact that Haman became so enraged when told of Mordecai's refusal to bow testifies to Haman's insecurity. Haman didn't measure his position by the admiration of many but rather by the rejection of one. This is the trap of man's approval. Haman's puffed-up pride was terribly unstable as evidenced by his reactive anger. If he had been truly fulfilled by the honor of others, there would be no room to be so quickly undone.

We think earning man's favor will satisfy, but instead it's so precarious that one negative reaction can become our tipping point. Our worth is only as good as our latest review. Haman was seated above all the other nobles, but one Jewish gatekeeper erased all that joy.

The irony of our online and celebrity generation is evidenced in the rising rates of depression and anxiety despite the constant ability to earn man's approval. The truth is that we are not made to be worshipped. If you aren't convinced of this, consider all the famous people who publicly enjoy the limelight and riches but struggle with private battles. While born with a hunger for glory, seeking it for ourselves is a misplaced endeavor. Only God can stand up to the worship and bear the heavy weight of it. When we seek to be worshipped, or when we worship other people, we are the creations stealing what is only fitting for the Creator.

The game to earn public approval is a trap. It can never be enough, no matter how great our power or popularity because there will always be naysayers. Their voices tend to drown out all others. The praise of man is a bottomless pit within us that cannot be filled by other people who are as equally flawed as we are. Satisfaction is a deeply sacred space that can only be filled by the delight of the God who created us.

A Life of Substance

In direct contrast to the arrogant Haman, Mordecai shows us what it is to be a faithful worshipper, true and unyielding. Mordecai, like Mamaw, played the long game. His eyes were fixed heavenward rather than to those around him as he both literally and figuratively stood firm in his small acts of faithfulness. Despite his humble status, Mordecai refused to bow down and pay honor to Haman.

Day after day.

Mordecai refused to comply, even when asked repeatedly (verse 4).

A righteous life is not built by huge, sweeping gestures and demonstrations of faith. Instead, a righteous life is built by steadfastly, day by day, choosing to surrender to obedience in the tiny and unseen acts of faith. A life of great faith is created gradually with a million minute by minute and day after day choices to look to God rather than to our circumstances.

• *What are you doing day after day to fix your eyes on God and his Word and bow to him in worship and fellowship?*

As we already know, Mordecai was well aware of the happenings at the palace. We saw in Esther 2:11 how Mordecai walked back and forth near the courtyard to keep tabs on Esther inside the palace. Esther 2:21-23 describes how Mordecai was strategically placed to learn of the plot against Ahasuerus, and he was not afraid to speak up to stop the plot against the king.

Mordecai was, indeed, a brave and bold man. He was certainly well aware of the risk that he took when he refused to bow to the powerful and prideful Haman. Though Haman acted like a bully, Mordecai seemed to view God as bigger than any person who came against him. Mordecai refused to operate out of fear, rightly placing his reverence for God over any fear of man.

• *How do you handle the constant struggle for man's approval? Have you become aware of the triggers that lead to anxiety or insecurity? What is your game plan to guard against these? How can you change your thought life?*

Where did Mordecai find this motivation to refuse to bow to Haman?

Do not make idols or set up an image or a sacred stone for

yourselves, and do not place a carved stone in your land to

bow before it. I am the Lord your God.

Leviticus 26:1 (NIV)

Love the Lord your God and keep his requirements, his decrees, his

laws and his commands always... Be careful, or you will be enticed

to turn away and worship other gods and bow down to them.

Deuteronomy 11:1, 16 (NIV)

Those who cling to worthless idols forfeit the grace that could be

theirs.

Jonah 2:8 (NET)

Mordecai's refusal to bow parallels the story of Shadrach, Meshach, and Abednego found in Daniel chapter 3. Those three Jewish exiles refused to bow to King Nebuchadnezzar's golden statue. They, too, enraged those in authority and were threatened with death because of their choice to worship God alone. Chronologically, King Nebuchadnezzar's reign was prior to that of Ahasuerus, so it stands to reason that Mordecai would have known the story of the three young Israelites who knelt only before their God.

One more relevant historical fact to consider regarding why Mordecai refused to bow is that Haman is noted in Esther to be an Agagite, which means he was an Amalekite from the line of King Agag. Generations of conflict between the Amalekites and the Israelites are cited within Exodus 17:16, Deuteronomy 25:17, and 1

118

Samuel 15. Haman's lineage alone put him at odds with the Jewish nation. Going further back, Mordecai, from the Israeli tribe of Benjamin, was a descendant of Jacob and Haman was a descendant of Esau, thus fulfilling the word of the Lord given to Rebekah in Genesis.

Two nations are in your womb, and two peoples from within you shall be divided; the one shall be stronger than the other, the older shall serve the younger.

Genesis 25:23

The fact that Haman was prideful and demanding surely added to Mordecai's resolve to defer his praise for God alone. Day after day, Mordecai made the choice, time and again, to be obedient to God and to serve the Holy God above all mankind, above all threat.

Choosing to obey God should bring an expectation of opposition. While living on Earth with our minds set on heaven, we can assume the world will push back. We shouldn't be surprised by those who come against us. Rather, we should be prepared for the fact that it will happen. Jesus himself was questioned by his own family. Some of them didn't believe he had divine purpose. He was misunderstood by his own disciples. He was continually opposed by the religious leaders who eventually succeeded to arrest, beat, flog, and crucify him. Look to this prophesy that Isaiah gave about Jesus:

He had no beauty or majesty to attract us to him,

nothing in his appearance that we should desire him.

He was despised and rejected by men,

a man of sorrows, and familiar with suffering.

Like one from whom men hide their faces

he was despised, and we esteemed him not.

Surely, he took up our infirmities

and carried our sorrows,

yet we considered him stricken by God,

smitten by him, and afflicted.

He was pierced for our transgressions,

he was crushed for our iniquities;

the punishment that brought us peace was upon him,

and by his wounds we are healed.

Isaiah 53:2b-5 (NIV)

This is the reality of our justified, sanctified, and eventually glorified lives through Christ. The world may despise us, but the Word tells us that healing, peace, and wholeness is ours because of Jesus.

But thanks be to God, who in Christ always leads us in triumphal procession, and through us spreads the fragrance of the knowledge of him everywhere. For we are the aroma of Christ to God among those who are being saved and among those who are perishing, to one a fragrance from death to death, to the other a fragrance from life to life. Who is sufficient for these things?

2 Corinthians 2:14-16 (NIV)

To some people, we "smell sweet" and are pleasing. To others, we are a stench. As opposition comes, we cope by fixing our gaze and intention squarely on our heavenly Father, following the way of Jesus. We remind ourselves that we are invited to banquet and feast on the eternal acceptance of the Holy God. We preach to ourselves that obedience to him trumps temporary pleasure and worldly acceptance. We boldly proclaim to our souls that our greatest reality is yet to come in the more glorious and better country of our eternity. We silence the voice of the accusations by shouting the TRUTH over them.

If the world hates you, keep in mind that it hated me first.

John 15:18 (NIV)

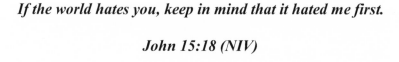

"I have told you these things, so that in me, you may have peace. In this world you will have trouble.

But take heart!

I have overcome the world."

John 16:33 (NIV)

The Importance of Discerning Your Influencers

Within Esther 3, the foolishness of the temperamental Haman is surpassed only by that of King Ahasuerus. This ruler of a vast kingdom, "successful" by the world's standards, simply believed all that Haman reported to him without asking any questions. Certainly, if not centered on Christ, the dynamics of our inner circles become carefully balanced upon the pride of those in power, requiring strategic stroking of egos. Haman knew exactly how to influence the ego of Ahasuerus, and the king blindly took the bait.

Fueled by emotion, Haman painted a half-truth and contorted deceits about the Jewish people, neither naming them specifically nor their number, withholding these facts as Jews represented a significant economic contribution to the kingdom of Ahasuerus. Instead, Haman portrayed these "enemies" as dangerous and despicable, certain to

123

bring widespread upheaval, thus mimicking the dire warning of the king's advisors regarding the fallout from Queen Vashti's behavior in Esther 1. The king was so inattentive and apparently so enamored by Haman that he did not investigate Haman's claims or seek clarification, but rather fell prey to acting out of fear.

The truth was Mordecai's refusal to bow to Haman posed no threat to the kingdom or the king's rule and reign. But, lacking discernment and wisdom, the king had given such a place of influence to Haman that he indiscriminately went along. Although Esther had been the wife of Ahasuerus for five years at this point and had gained great favor by the king, it wasn't enough to guard Ahasuerus against the influence of Haman.

Keep your heart with all vigilance,

for from it flow the springs of life.

Proverbs 4:23

Ahasuerus then acted on Haman's warnings by consulting the soothsayers to find the lucky day for the proposed massacre of these "dangerous people" through the casting the lot, or the Pur. Next, Ahasuerus handed his signet ring to Haman. In so doing, Ahasuerus gave Haman authority and decision-making power to issue and verify irrevocable decrees. Ahasuerus' motivation to such blind allegiance with Haman doesn't seem financially motivated, as he refused the promised treasury that would come from the plunder of those massacred, which is equivalent to $55 million in today's marketplace.

Ahasuerus simply failed to guard his heart and watch with discernment for influencers in his circle. His foolishness granted Haman the ability to call for the destruction of an entire people group because of the personal insult from one person.

Aren't we all inclined to do this? One little thing goes awry, and we suddenly feel overwhelmed. We allow it fester in our minds and relive and rehearse it over and again until it grows like a consuming wildfire. We lose the ability to be objective and don't even recognize that our emotions are creating a monumental issue that doesn't reflect the reality.

We assign the thoughts or opinions of one person to all the people we know. We focus more on the wounds from others than we do the wounds of Jesus that cover all sins. We ignore God's instruction that it is to our glory to overlook an offense (Proverbs 19:11). We cuddle these offenses like a security blanket, never realizing how damaging it can be when we deny ourselves the freedom that extending forgiveness could bring. We allow the influence of others and our emotions to direct our actions rather than guarding our hearts against such foolishness by growing in biblical wisdom and discernment.

• *To whom, or to what emotion, do you give your signet ring, meaning your decision-making? Whose advice or what feelings are you giving power to by granting them the throne of your heart and mind?*

The Sovereign God

When the king and Haman cast the lot, it seemed that things were going exactly as Haman hoped, having secured the "lucky" date for the destruction of all Jews to occur on the thirteenth day of the last month, known as Adar.

But God. Upon closer examination, we can discover how God was actually weaving it all together.

Haman and Ahasuerus had no concept of how God is ultimately in control.

The lot is cast into the lap,

but its every decision is from the Lord.

Proverbs 16:33 (NIV)

No one is immune to plot twists in life. It's easy to look at the trouble in front of us as a colossal threat. When this occurs, we can consider how David handled his own literal giant. Prior to his showdown with Goliath, God did not prepare David by ensuring he was a skilled warrior with battleground experience. Instead, God prepared David through years spent tending the sheep and learning who his Shepherd was.

That is how we face our giants. Day after day, we choose time with God, listening to him, learning who he is, and gaining knowledge of the truths of him. We grow these truths in our minds and hearts to let them take hold with deep roots so that on the day of trouble we view our emotions and circumstance within the shadow of our Sovereign God. This allows us to withstand the storms, bending but not breaking.

We make it a habit to recall how God has been faithful before so that we can build hope and courage when our very lives depend on him being faithful again.

Haman thought he had it well in hand. In hindsight, we realize that God allowed the lot to be cast for a day that was eleven months away, giving his people ample time to prepare and respond. In our lives, we can look at the day of destruction coming, or we can focus on the Sovereign God who is the Keeper of all time. Through my own experience I've learned that he is the God who intersects our stories, even with the plot twists, and we can trust that he will remain the Author and Perfecter of our faith to hold us firmly through the turmoil.

Look for the "Unseen" on the Fringe

The third chapter of Esther closes with this: "The king and Haman sat down to drink, but the city of Susa was bewildered." As the death warrant for all Jews was sent with haste to all of the 127 provinces in every language, Ahasuerus and Haman sat down in the palace to have a drink. Perhaps they were drowning any sense of guilt, or maybe they were toasting with glee about what they've just decided.

In the meantime, chaos and weeping erupted with the news. Bible commentaries note that the Jews were a peaceful people and the bewilderment of the kingdom surely included compassionate non-Jews.₁ Various translations of Esther 3:15 say that the citizens of Susa were reeling and confused.

We can be quick to judge the callous hearts of Ahasuerus and Haman as they toasted to the coming massacre—except that we are often just like them. We are merrily oblivious to the plight of those around us. In our own homes and cities, there are those facing hard times. In our world, we in the West are the elite and the rich, while most of the world lives on $2 a day or less.₂

All around us, there are those unseen who are confused, bewildered, and facing doom. We so easily turn a blind eye and raise our glasses around our plentiful kitchens, never considering those who are despairing. We compare ourselves to those above us financially and ignore those below us.

We need to put down our glasses and be intentional to actually look for and serve others in need. Most of us can easily take a hit on our indulgences or our time to help leverage our resources for those who need them. All of us can afford to be more intentional to enter the sufferings of people around us.

It's really not hard to move toward the unseen. As we keep our gaze on God, we ask him for eyes to see those who are bewildered in life. We pick up the phone and call them, considering tangible ways to ease their burdens.

On a more global scale, we throw our weight behind all the incredible organizations and ministries who seek to even the playing field. We smile at the grumpy cashier. We pay for the groceries of the lady behind us. We sit in the hospital waiting room. We fold the laundry of the tired mama with sick kids.

Loving others well. That's the gospel call for a life well lived. We realize how we are so like Ahasuerus and Haman, and then we move out of our comfort zones to bow our lives to worship God and serve his people.

Response to Esther 3

The Word of God is meant to transform and call us to action. Take some time to consider the questions below and write out your responses.

• *What do you do on a daily basis that is motivated by earning the approval of others or to gauge the opinion of others? Do you feel the sting of "scarcity" – that someone else's success limits your own ability for it?*

• *Whose opinion matters most to you? Whose criticism unravels you?*

• *To whom do you give a position of influence that leads you away from God? What are some areas that you could stand to change through biblical wisdom and instruction?*

• *Who do you have influence within your day-to-day life? Do you use that influence for godly wisdom and biblical living? If not, how can you change that?*

• *What are you currently facing that feels like the luck of the draw? What feels out of your control? Begin to pray that God will help you grow your belief in His ability to turn the circumstances for your eternal good. Mark 9:24 is a favorite verse of mine to pray for such*

things: "I do believe you can _____. Help my unbelief!"

• *What is ONE thing you can do this week to reach into the lives of*

the "unseen" or those on the margins of your life who are facing

trials?

The Truths of Esther 3

Let's wrap up this section of Scripture by considering these three

elements.

1—Adoration of God from Esther 3

- You are the One whose opinion and approval matter the

  most.

- You are the God who calls us to obedience day after day.

- You are the God who is bigger than and above any fear of man.

- You are the God who alone is worthy of us bowing to honor and praise.

- You are the God above all mankind and all creation and all things.

- You are the God who rules and reigns, even when trouble comes.

- You are the God who calls for my obedience, even when it comes with risks.

- You are the God to whom we cry when trouble comes.

- You are the God who sees, even when I feel unseen.

2—Affirmation of Our Gospel Identity from Esther 3

- I have a purpose in God's kingdom, exactly where I am, every day.

- I am daily in God's care.

- I am equipped to stand firm for God through God's power, grace, and love and through the Holy Spirit within me.

- I am a worshipper of God.

- I am being held by God, even when it doesn't feel like it.

3—Actions to Take from Esther 3

- I need not live for man's empty praise.

- I am to stand firm for God, day after day, bowing to him alone.

- I am to not be surprised by troubles or opposition.

- I am not to act out of anger.

- I am not to act out of fear of man but out of holy fear and reverence for God.

- I am to be discerning about those who influence my heart and thoughts.

- I am to run to God for protection and refuge.

- I am to remind myself of the truths of God and his Word when things feel awful and hard.

- I am to preach the truth of how God has fought for me in the past to inform me in current battles.

- I am to live out the rhythm of the gospel by loving the unseen, replicating how God has loved me.

Conclusion of Esther 3

May we be encouraged by the example of Mordecai. Even ordinary, second-class citizens can be bold to choose obedience to God despite all opposition or danger. It's not that Mordecai was superhuman. It's that he turned his heart repeatedly toward the supernatural God whom he knew could do the impossible, day after day. Mordecai chose God in the unimportant and daily grind, and it equipped him to choose God when it was hard to do so. That's how we live faithfully and that's how we face the giants of circumstance that bring a sense of doom.

ESTHER 4

In every province to which the edict and order of the king came,

there was great mourning among the Jews, with fasting, weeping,

and wailing. Many lay in sackcloth and ashes.

Esther 4:3

...relief and deliverance will rise for the Jews from another place...

Esther 4:14

"...And if I perish, I perish."

Esther 4:16b

Esther 4, *English Standard Version*

Esther Agrees to Help the Jews

4 When Mordecai learned all that had been done, Mordecai tore his clothes and put on sackcloth and ashes, and went out into the midst of the city, and he cried out with a loud and bitter cry. 2 He went up to the entrance of the king's gate, for no one was allowed to enter the king's gate clothed in sackcloth. 3 And in every province, wherever the king's command and his decree reached, there was great mourning among the Jews, with fasting and weeping and lamenting, and many of them lay in sackcloth and ashes.

4 When Esther's young women and her eunuchs came and told her, the queen was deeply distressed. She sent garments to clothe Mordecai, so that he might take off his sackcloth, but he would not accept them. 5 Then Esther called for Hathach, one of the king's eunuchs, who had been appointed to attend her, and ordered him to go to Mordecai to learn what this was and why it was. 6 Hathach went out to Mordecai in the open square of the city in front of the king's gate, 7 and Mordecai told him all that had happened to him, and the exact sum of money that Haman had promised to pay

into the king's treasuries for the destruction of the Jews. 8 Mordecai also gave him a copy of the written decree issued in Susa for their destruction, that he might show it to Esther and explain it to her and command her to go to the king to beg his favor and plead with him on behalf of her people. 9 And Hathach went and told Esther what Mordecai had said. 10 Then Esther spoke to Hathach and commanded him to go to Mordecai and say, 11 "All the king's servants and the people of the king's provinces know that if any man or woman goes to the king inside the inner court without being called, there is but one law—to be put to death, except the one to whom the king holds out the golden scepter so that he may live. But as for me, I have not been called to come in to the king these thirty days."

12 And they told Mordecai what Esther had said. 13 Then Mordecai told them to reply to Esther, "Do not think to yourself that in the king's palace you will escape any more than all the other Jews. 14 For if you keep silent at this time, relief and deliverance will rise for the Jews from another place, but you and your father's house will perish. And who knows whether you have not come to the kingdom for such a time as this?" 15 Then Esther told them to reply to Mordecai, 16 "Go,

gather all the Jews to be found in Susa, and hold a fast on my behalf, and do not eat or drink for three days, night or day. I and my young women will also fast as you do. Then I will go to the king, though it is against the law, and if I perish, I perish." 17 Mordecai then went away and did everything as Esther had ordered him.

THE DAY OF DEVASTATION

Esther 4

The most pivotal moment in my life happened when my calculus homework was interrupted during my senior year of high school. I was sitting in a hospital waiting room as the surgeons removed my dad's cancer. All the test results indicated that the surgery would be successful, which was familiar territory for our family. Eight years prior, my dad's colon cancer was removed through surgery.

Yet only partway through this surgery, the surgeon called my family into the hallway.

"The liver biopsy gave a false negative. The cancer has spread all throughout the liver. There's nothing we can do. We are closing him up now. He has three to six months to live."

I can't remember if he said anything else. I only remember the gasps and sobs and confusion from all of my family members. As we huddled in a very public hallway, having just been given the worst news of my life, it felt as though the surgeon dropped the bomb and left us with the collateral damage. I remember hearing crying, but, honestly, I'm not sure if it was my own or someone else's or maybe just everyone's.

If ever there was a time in my life to fall to my knees and weep, this was it.

The Art of Grieving

It may seem strange to admit that I'm jealous of the Jewish mourning traditions—unless you've ever experienced a time of devastation. In those despairing times, the idea of a cultural norm and expected reaction such as wailing bitterly, tearing at your clothes, and putting on sackcloth and ashes can offer a sense of comfort.

The closest ritual we have is candlelit gatherings during times of loss. Yet one of the things I admire is that the Jewish tradition doesn't call for silence and signs of hope, but rather it allows the full expression of deep sorrow. The Jewish tradition calls for public mourning and for company to sit "Shiva" with the grieving for a seven-day mourning period. ı

Grieving is an art with no manual, no instructors, few classes, and often no company. We tend to respond to the pain of others much as Esther did with news of Mordecai's weeping. We want those who are grieving to change out of their sackcloth. The fact is it's uncomfortable to be around hurting people. It's not convenient or easy to sit with someone who's feeling anguished.

We do well to lean into the images of grieving from Esther 4 as the chapter describes sackcloth, ashes, loud and bitter cries, mourning, fasting, weeping, lamenting, and being deeply distressed. Mordecai offers us a beautiful example of a man who was unashamed to not only fully vent his grief but to also boldly identify as one who was condemned. Lest we forget, this death sentence was issued for all the Jews because of the choice of this one Jew.

In the face of utter destruction, the Jewish people denied themselves the comfort of food and even their own beds as they fasted and laid in their sackcloth and ashes.

• *When someone you know is in a similar state of mind, do you tend to remain isolated and removed from the tears, as Esther was within the comforts and walls of the palace? Or do you reach out directly, even going to sit quietly with the hurting?*

Rejoice with those who rejoice; weep with those who weep.

Romans 12:15

In order to mourn with those in mourning, we have to know why they are mourning, which requires intentional effort. The Bible outlines how difficult times give an opportunity for the gospel rhythm to be replicated. God comforts us so that we can be comforters for others.

Blessed be the God and Father of our Lord Jesus Christ, the Father of mercies and God of all comfort, who comforts us in all our affliction, so that we may be able to comfort those who are in any affliction, with the comfort with which we ourselves are comforted by God. For as we share abundantly in Christ's sufferings, so through Christ we share abundantly in comfort too.

2 Corinthians 1:3-5

Comforting those facing afflictions, despite how awkward it feels to us, is not a suggestion but a command for the body of Christ.

Carry each other's burdens, and in this way,

you will fulfill the law of Christ.

Galatians 6:2 (NIV)

The reality is that we don't need to have the answers or to cheer up the hurting. People are afraid to say anything because they don't want to remind the hurting people of their pain. Yet I can assure you that hurting people don't forget their pain. To truly be a great comfort, we actually don't have to say anything.

We grieve with those who grieve by bravely choosing to join in their sadness within close proximity. We don't abandon the hurting, and we don't assume someone else is checking in. We do what it takes to remind ourselves to text them every few days or call them regularly. We mark our calendar with the one month, three-month, six-month, and one-year anniversaries of the loss so that we can remind them they aren't forgotten.

We carry the burden and grieve with the grieving simply by listening, showing up with Kleenex® and a meal, seeking to know how they're coping, being inconvenienced, being interrupted, and being available.

My all-time favorite movie is *Steel Magnolias*. Along with the memorable one-liners, I love the portrayal of community as the main characters respond to a death. Two of the women grocery shop for the grieving family and another profoundly processes the loss with her own husband. The best scene, however, is when the women gather just after the funeral. Like so many of us searching for the right response, they offer clichés until the grieving mother becomes unraveled. They stay near as she gives full vent to her emotions, even following her as she wails, and then they offer up the grumpiest among them to be a punching bag.

Compassion is going to the hard places with someone and choosing to be mindful that their position is exponentially harder. Compassion is being a safe place for the sacred season of lament and grief, no matter how awkward, messy, or uncomfortable. Compassion is remembering that you have a Father who is the God of all comfort and he comforts us so that we can comfort others.

The Miraculous Scepter

My dad's battle with cancer and his subsequent death brought some of the biggest gifts for my faith journey. Within my sorrow, I learned the importance of being honest and authentic in my relationship with God. Up until then, I placed God within a box of assumptions, believing that he had a majesty requiring isolation from my despair and unpleasantries, likening God to someone like King Ahasuerus who allowed no one to enter his gates in sackcloth. I played the part of court jester due to my insecurity about his affection for me and my position before him, as if I were Esther who hadn't been summoned in more than thirty days.

Growing up in a home that avoided expressing and processing difficult feelings, I projected this into my relationship with the Lord, thinking I needed to hide my dark feelings from God. I felt prayer required me to be a good Christian girl who remained full of positive attitudes and pleasantries. Anything less or anything resembling questioning was to be squashed.

• Do you have any misconceptions or presumptions about God that have been or are now roadblocks to intimacy with him?

The original Hebrew word in Esther 4:11 used to describe the death sentence for entering the king's presence unsummoned is the same word from Daniel 2:5 that describes how Nebuchadnezzar would tear the men from limb to limb and leave their homes in ruins if they couldn't interpret his dreams. 2 Coming unannounced, much less in sackcloth, was indeed life or death for anyone in Susa.

It's taken me decades to realize that, while I grew up knowing Jesus loves me, I didn't actually believe the depths of his love and acceptance. I struggled to believe that I am simultaneously fully known, with all my faults, *and* fully loved. I compared my approach to God to how people were to enter the courtroom of this earthly king, Ahasuerus, with a formality and acceptance that I didn't possess. These were not conscious thoughts, but my heart attitude definitely wrestled with and acted from legalism.

I never realized the miracle of the golden scepter pictured in Esther 4 until I stormed into the throne room of God wearing my sackcloth and ashes and giving full voice to my deep sorrow. Since that anguished moment on my bedroom floor at college, I've been growing in my understanding of God's accessibility and holiness, as well as expanding my knowledge and belief in grace.

Grace is the miracle of the golden scepter. Grace isn't just a one-time transaction offered through the cross, but it's an ongoing outpouring that began when the temple's veil to the Holy of Holies was ripped on Good Friday as Jesus died, granting direct access to the King. You see, Jesus is the golden scepter. Jesus paid the death sentence required to commune with the triune God without need for sacrifice or priestly intercession, and Jesus is why we can enjoy the safety net of grace to approach God continually in every circumstance.

Since then we have a great high priest who has passed through the heavens, Jesus, the Son of God, let us hold fast our confession. For we do not have a high priest who is unable to sympathize with our weaknesses, but one who in every respect has been tempted as we are, yet without sin. Let us then with confidence draw near to the throne of grace, that we may receive mercy and find grace to help in time of need.

Hebrews 4:14-16

Like David in Psalms and Jeremiah in Lamentations, we can lament to our Lord. He's big enough to take our questions, though he owes us no explanations. If he were small enough to understand, then he wouldn't be big enough to worship. We may never know his purposes in our pain, but he wants us to process our pain with him.

He can handle all our feelings, fears, bad days, and grief. He knows our thoughts from afar anyway (Psalm 139), and he requires no pretenses from us. God is the safest place where we can run when we are overwhelmed with emotion or when awful things happen. Even more astonishing is that in times when we can't find words for our deep emotions, the Bible offers these amazing promises.

In the same way, the Spirit helps us in our weakness. We do not know what we ought to pray for, but the Spirit himself intercedes for us with groans that words cannot express.
And he who searches our hearts knows the mind of the Spirit, because the Spirit intercedes for the saints in accordance with God's will.
Romans 8:26-27 (NIV)

But because Jesus lives forever, he has a permanent priesthood, therefore he is able to save completely those who come to God through him, because he always lives to intercede for them.
Hebrews 7:24-25 (NIV)

To intercede means to plead, petition, or mediate for someone.3 In other words, as followers of Jesus, we have the Holy Spirit within us, praying for us with groans too deep for words. As if that's not enough, the book of Hebrews promises that Jesus himself is pleading with the Father on our behalf. We need no engraved invitation, and he has no dress code. Our sackcloth and ashes are welcomed because Jesus robes us in his righteousness.

Have mercy on me, Lord, for I am faint;

heal me, Lord, for my bones are in agony.

My soul is in deep anguish. How long, Lord, how long?

… I am worn out from my groaning.

All night long I flood my bed with weeping

and drench my couch with tears.

My eyes grow weak with sorrow;… the Lord has heard my cry for

mercy; the Lord accepts my prayer.

Psalm 6:2-3, 6-7a, 9 (NIV)

I remember my affliction and my wandering, the bitterness and the gall. I well remember them, and my soul is downcast within me. Yet this I call to mind and therefore have hope: Because of the Lord's great love, we are not consumed, for his compassions never fail. They are new every morning; great is your faithfulness.

Lamentations 3:19-23 (NIV)

The Response to the Threat

The transition from Mordecai's weeping to his command for Esther's actions marks a juncture that could be mistaken for a callous or hardened attitude within Mordecai toward Esther. However, let's not forget. Mordecai raised Esther as his very own, loving her as a daughter. He knew the risk to Esther's life just for approaching the king. He was, in fact, so aware of their position as exiles in Susa that he had forbidden Esther from revealing her true nationality.

This is the cautious and concerned cousin who, every day for twelve months, walked back and forth at the gate, waiting for any word of Esther's well-being from within the palace. His sudden boldness with Esther had nothing to do with a lack of concern for her welfare.

I believe that the loving and doting cousin of Esther dared to be so bold for one reason only.

Mordecai's confidence in the covenant and Word of God was bigger than his fears.

The original Hebrew word Mordecai uses for "her people" in Esther 4:8 is a word meaning "the remnant will return" or "those spared to inhabit or to be settled, dwell, or stay." 4 This Hebrew word is used throughout Isaiah's prophecies regarding the Jewish people who would be the remnant of Jerusalem and the remnant of Judah. In other words, Mordecai used a very specific form of the word "people" to indicate those whom God had promised to preserve from Babylonian captivity.

Thus, Mordecai's lamenting was informed by the covenant promises of God regarding the future remnant, and this knowledge emboldened him to ask Esther to act courageously despite grave danger. Mordecai chose to let the certainty of God and his promises speak louder than any fear or doubt, even if he and Esther were not to be part of the remnant preserved.

Though King Ahasuerus had issued an edict that was legally unchangeable, Mordecai pinned all his hope on the greater King whose Word trumps any words or actions or intentions of man. Mordecai looked eye to eye with what seemed to be a certain destruction of his people because of the resolve that his God had the final word.

The Way to Build Belief

Belief. We cower in fear as we face the battles in our life because we allow our unbelief to make our temporary circumstances bigger than the eternal God. We find the ability to expect God's deliverance when we believe God for every word he says. Rather than praying for God to become big enough to match our needs, we must pray for our belief to grow big enough to match our God. We may feel like the Israeli soldiers quaking in our armor as we face our Goliaths, but we have a God who is the slayer of all giants.

Nothing in our lives, from circumstance to emotion, builds belief in God without great intention. Mordecai was an ordinary man who chose to follow the faith of his fathers in a foreign land after the horrific destruction of Jerusalem that had led to exile. I believe that he was able to respond to the threat, not as one remarkable proclamation of faith, but because of a well-established habit along the way to remind himself of God's promises and his track record from past generations.

Belief that faces down our darkest days with confidence is grown gradually, over time, in the seemingly ordinary acts of choosing to read our Bible, to pray, to go to church, and to worship. This kind of deep faith with great fruit happens in tiny, nearly invisible steps of a thousand decisions to fill our minds with the excellencies of God's character. Continually preaching truth to our souls instead of listening to our emotions eventually produces a transformation in how we respond, and it cures our tendency to react. The habit of elevating God continually in our thoughts can silence our bullying emotions as we build a healthier God-esteem.

The Importance of Remembering

Mordecai and Esther are not any different from us. Their stories aren't about an overnight or unusual faith but are about broken, regular people who wrestled with life by refocusing their belief on an extraordinary God. When all that we can see is danger or trouble, we go back and preach to our hurting and fearful selves that God is for us. When we have no song of deliverance to sing because we see no way out, we borrow a song from the lives of other people. As a devout Jewish man, we can assume that Mordecai knew God's Word, perhaps not from writings, but from oral history passed down to him.

Mordecai knew that God had promised his forefather Abraham that he would make his descendants as numerous as the grains of sand and that God made an everlasting covenant with him that all nations would be blessed through his offspring (Genesis 12).

He knew that Joseph was sold into Egyptian slavery by his brothers and that what man meant for evil God used for good to save the Israelite nation from famine (Genesis 50:19-20).

Mordecai knew that the Israelite people prospered so greatly in Egypt that they became a threat. He knew that the Egyptian pharaoh enslaved the Israelites and then ordered the baby boys to be killed to stop the population growth. And he knew that two Hebrew midwives refused to obey the pharaoh's orders, thereby sparing one certain little boy named Moses (Exodus 1).

He knew that God dried up the Red Sea so that the Israeli nation could walk on dry land into safety, even as the Egyptian army closed in on them (Exodus 14).

He knew how his ancestors listened and obeyed God and then turned to idol worship again and again. He knew God would allow the Jewish people to be defeated and held captive because of their disobedience. And then, when they cried out to God, he would send someone to save them.

Mordecai knew that the Israelites had been brought into Babylonian captivity because of their defiant idol worship. He knew that three young men before him refused to bow to a golden statue and were thrown into a fiery furnace heated up seven times hotter than usual. He knew that Shadrach, Meshach, and Abednego declared that their God could save them and even if he didn't, they would still believe he was good (Daniel 3).

He knew that as those men entered the furnace, the fire scorched the soldiers who threw them in, and then King Nebuchadnezzar suddenly saw a fourth man in the fire "glowing like a god" (Daniel 3:25).

Mordecai knew that when we are thrown into the fire ourselves, God goes with us.

He knew that those three young men not only walked out of that furnace alive but that when they came out, "they did not even smell like smoke" (Daniel 3:27).

When Mordecai was put to the test, at the risk of losing his own life, the lives of his people, and his beloved Esther, uncertainty was staring him down. Yet he could build his faith by calling to mind the certainty of what he knew from the past, falling on a healthy and strong God-esteem to hold him up during his anguish.

He knew the stories of the Jewish people before him. He knew their songs of deliverance. He knew their stories of rescue, and he knew the promises and character of God. He was certain of his identity as one of God's people, and he was convinced that God had an unseen kingdom purpose beyond the visible circumstances.

The Call to Rise Up

We can know what is true all day long, but in our times of torment, our ability to find a footing will depend on which is bigger - our belief or our unbelief.

He [Mordecai] sent back this answer: "Do not think that because you are in the king's house you alone of all the Jews will escape. For if you remain silent at this time, relief and deliverance for the Jews will arise from another place but you and your father's family will perish. And who knows but that you have come to royal position for such a time as this?"

Esther 4:13-14 (NIV)

A robust belief in God allowed Mordecai to look beyond the kingdom of Susa to see the kingdom of God. Through this kingdom focus, he reminds Esther to do the same, serving their God rather than preserving her own life through disobedience.

Whoever finds his life will lose it, and

whoever loses his life for my sake will find it.

Matthew 10:39

To live every day with a certainty that we are strategically placed for divine purpose is to live surrendered to the daily opportunities that God gives us to serve our generation.

And he made from one man every nation of mankind to live on all

the face of the earth, having determined allotted periods and the

boundaries of their dwelling place,

that they should seek God, and perhaps feel their way toward him

and find him. Yet he is actually not far from each one of us.

Acts 17:26-27

God intends for us to wake up every morning with a confidence that every person we encounter, every moment, and every resource we have can be leveraged for eternal purposes.

The Full Context of Verse 14

One of the biggest stumbling blocks to building our belief is failing to study the Bible in full context from cover to cover. The most quoted verse from the entire book of Esther is verse 14 of chapter 4, although usually quoted only in part: "…And who knows but that you have come to royal position for such a time as this?" The problem with coffee-mug Christianity is that we miss the actual meaning.

The marvelous intention of Esther 4:14 is not that we feel puffed up by having a purpose or place, but that we feel humbled by the invitation to partner with God in all that he will accomplish. It's not "for such a time as this," but rather that he is the God who will bring relief and deliverance. He does not need our help in that. Yet he dares to so boldly invite us in to be part of such relief and deliverance. Our Western Christianity likes to see ourselves as the main character and the object of the lesson. This prideful approach numbs us to the bewildering reality that a God who does not need for anything chooses to let us be part of his ongoing relief and deliverance.

We tend to love the warm, fuzzy feeling about what we can do for God, but it makes us blind to what he has done for us. We have absolutely nothing to boast about except for his grace. How arrogant we are to feel good about what we can do for God, for such a time as this, thereby blinded to his startling partnership with us. The reality, as preached by JR Vassar, is that "anything but grace as our identity will never measure up because we will be always riding the waves" and "when anything grips our heart but the glory and grace of God, it will drive us mad because our idols will fail us." 5

Purpose in the Mundane

What God dares to invite us to participate in with him will likely never look like what Esther was asked to do. Yes, we may be part of something monumental and noteworthy, or our lives may be a calling to the tedious and mundane. We can never discount that an obedient heart in the daily things is being used for the eternal, unseen kingdom of God. Bowing our hearts to be awed by God's inclusion of us will grant us the ability to fully rise to every opportunity.

The Posture of Power

Like Esther and Mordecai, we find courage for whatever comes at us when we are surrendered to God. At the beginning of Esther 3, Mordecai refused to kneel before Haman. This crucial chapter 4 of Esther ends with Esther, Mordecai, and the entire Jewish population in Susa now rightly kneeling before God at their most critical hour (Esther 4:15-17).

Before Esther risked her life, she began by being still before God through prayer and fasting. Prayer is how we best prepare for and complete life's battles of either epic or daily proportions. Like building our belief in God, building a powerful prayer life comes incrementally with regular habits of adoration, confession, petition, and listening. We invest in our relationship with God through regular communication just we do with the people we hold most dear, rather than treating him as our 911 dispatcher or our genie in a bottle.

Fixing her eyes squarely on God enabled Esther to proclaim, "And if I perish, I perish" (Esther 4:16). Esther's choices were either a possible death by her husband or a more certain death orchestrated by her enemy, Haman. She chose obedience to God, not out of confidence in the outcome or her own ability, but out of surrender to the God who held her firmly either way.

During those three days of prayer, she looked beyond her circumstance to see God more clearly. Surely, she was resolved that obedience was hers and the results were God's.

Faith is choosing to believe God is who he said he is and who he has been even when we can't see what's ahead of us. It's training our eyes to look to the wonders of God beyond the hurdles right in front of us.

Response to Esther 4

The Word of God is meant to transform and call us to action. Take some time to consider the questions below and write out your responses.

• *Who is grieving or struggling that you know, and how might you grieve with them?*

• *Is there something you're facing that you haven't approached God's throne about in prayer or that you've neglected to pray about earnestly though it fills your thoughts? If so, take time to pray about that right now, or write a letter to God to journal out your prayer.*

• *Think about the people and places where God has placed you and dared to invite you to his purposes, though you are not needed. Consider how you can be part of revealing Jesus to those people and places. How can you be part of his rescue of others? Ask God to reveal to you the magnitude of his invitation to partner with him and ask that he make his purposes clear to you daily for "such a time as this."*

• *Who can you impact and show God's love and light to every day as you go about your day? Who can you tell about God's story in your life?*

• How can you use your time, talents, and position for the kingdom of God?

• Who can you partner with in prayer?

• What stories from the Bible or your own family history give you strength and encourage you?

The Truths of Esther 4

Let's wrap up this section of Scripture by considering these three elements.

1—Adoration of God from Esther 4

- You are the God to whom we can wail and cry.

- You are the God who hears our heartaches.

- You are the God who goes through our weeping with us.

- You are the God who welcomes us through your gates, even in our "sackcloth and ashes."

- You are the God who is a safe place for our emotions.

- You are the God who gives us the Holy Spirit within us to intercede for us as our Counselor.

- You are the God whose Son lives to intercede for us at the right hand of your throne.

- You are the God of all comfort and compassion.

- You are the covenant God who is always near and promises to never forsake us.

- You are the God who has a plan and purpose for my life and eternity.

- You are the God who is bigger than any trouble I face.

- You are the God above all earthly kings and circumstances.

- You are the God of deliverance and rescue.

- You are the God who is the Ancient of Days with an eternal kingdom.

2—Affirmation of Our Gospel Identity from Esther 4

- I am able to be honest with God.

- I am never alone in my sorrow or struggles.

- I am loved and heard as a child of the heavenly Father.

- I am held by God through every hard day, even when it doesn't feel like it.

- I am uniquely positioned within God's plans for his people.

- I am invited to partner with God for his kingdom purposes.

- I am within the grip of the Almighty God through every circumstance.

3—Actions to Take from Esther 4

- I am to be honest and authentic with God, and I can lament to him, going to him as my refuge.

- I am to read and pray Scripture in all seasons.

- I am to seek God in all my troubles.

- I am to be moved by other's distress and mourn with those who mourn.

- I am to show God's comfort to others.

- I am to call to mind who God is, his promises, and his past deeds to help me find strength.

- I am to believe God for every word he says.

- I am to confess the sin of my unbelief that tries to rule my emotions and life.

- I am to remind myself of the truths of God and his Word when things feel awful and hard.

- I am to preach the truth of how God has fought for me in the past to encourage me in current battles.

- I am to refocus my eyes on the eternity to come during the hardest times on Earth.

- I am to pray first, act second.

- I am to pray with others and for others and ask them to do the same for me.

Conclusion of Esther 4

When we consider the millions of ways that God has shown who he is throughout history and in the promises of the Bible, we find strength to confidently believe God is for us.

This is why we should regularly tell the stories of how we see God working in our own lives. People need to hear them; they need to borrow our songs of deliverance until their own lyrics are written. The Bible commands us to proclaim his good deeds as one way to bring him glory.

God has a plan for his people, for this world, for mankind, and for all history. He does not need us to accomplish it, as Mordecai pointed out to Esther. Yet he dares to invite us to be part of his kingdom purpose because of who he is and not because of who we are. God lets us become part of his story as we allow him to write each chapter of our life day after day, surrendered to follow his way.

Never doubt that you have a part in God's plan for God's people. Never cease to be awed that the God of all creation, who spoke the world into existence with his voice and who reigns on his throne above all, chooses to invite you to find your identity in him as your King and to use your life to be part of his kingdom purpose.

ESTHER 5

On the third day Esther put on her royal robes and stood....

Esther 5:1a

Esther 5, *English Standard Version*

Esther Prepares a Banquet

5 On the third day Esther put on her royal robes and stood in the inner court of the king's palace, in front of the king's quarters, while the king was sitting on his royal throne inside the throne room opposite the entrance to the palace. 2 And when the king saw Queen Esther standing in the court, she won favor in his sight, and he held out to Esther the golden scepter that was in his hand. Then Esther approached and touched the tip of the scepter. 3 And the king said to her, "What is it, Queen Esther? What is your request? It shall be given you, even to the half of my kingdom." 4 And Esther said, "If it please the king, let the king and Haman come today to a feast that I have prepared for the king." 5 Then the king said, "Bring Haman quickly, so that we may do as Esther has asked." So the king and Haman came to the feast that Esther had prepared. 6 And as they were drinking wine after the feast, the king said to Esther, "What is your wish? It shall be granted you. And what is your request? Even to the half of my kingdom, it shall be fulfilled." 7 Then Esther answered, "My wish and my request is: 8 If I have found favor in the

sight of the king, and if it please the king to grant my wish and fulfill my request, let the king and Haman come to the feast that I will prepare for them, and tomorrow I will do as the king has said."

Haman Plans to Hang Mordecai

9 And Haman went out that day joyful and glad of heart. But when Haman saw Mordecai in the king's gate, that he neither rose nor trembled before him, he was filled with wrath against Mordecai. 10 Nevertheless, Haman restrained himself and went home, and he sent and brought his friends and his wife Zeresh. 11 And Haman recounted to them the splendor of his riches, the number of his sons, all the promotions with which the king had honored him, and how he had advanced him above the officials and the servants of the king. 12 Then Haman said, "Even Queen Esther let no one but me come with the king to the feast she prepared. And tomorrow also I am invited by her together with the king. 13 Yet all this is worth nothing to me, so long as I see Mordecai the Jew sitting at the king's gate." 14 Then his wife Zeresh and all his friends said to him, "Let a gallows fifty cubits high be made, and in the morning tell the king to

have Mordecai hanged upon it. Then go joyfully with the king to the

feast." This idea pleased Haman, and he had the gallows made.

BATTLE READY
Esther 5

It was the Friday evening at the beginning of spring break when the teacher called to request a parent conference. The kick in the gut came when she said the math teacher actually requested the entire fourth grade team to meet with my husband and myself, although he refused to place the call, requiring the homeroom teacher to handle it.

In hindsight all these years later, I should have politely deferred the call and instead made direct contact with the teacher who "was frustrated to the point of having no answers." Had this teacher been unknown to me, I might have understood his deferment to the homeroom teacher. However, since he taught our oldest son, I felt confused that he didn't fall back on our established relationship and that he'd made no effort to reach out before he felt it necessary to call in the whole team.

Through a series of lessons, with trial and error, I've learned more about acting as my children's advocate. If I knew then what I now know, I would have been more prepared and informed about the emotional, behavioral, and classroom needs of a child who has been identified as gifted and talented. The phone call that day confirmed my suspicion that there was a tendency to react and place blame as if my son were a problem to fix rather than a child to be understood.

I at least had the wherewithal to insist the gifted and talented teacher be present to help advocate. Beyond that, I felt the familiar ache that moms feel when our children are judged. It can be a lonely place to parent a child that others misunderstand or can't relate to for whatever reason.

That particular phone call and the upcoming meeting became a crossroads in my parenting. By the grace of God, spring break provided a good two weeks to prepare. My mama bear reaction was quieted through the gift of time, and my frustration and worry led me to a surrendered prayer for wisdom.

Biblical counsel won out as my heart softened to embrace the opportunity to handle it as God would have me. Instead of reacting to the criticisms, I was going to lead with grace. When the day came, my husband and I walked in feeling a peace only prayer and humility can bring. I had my outline and talking points. I stood at the door to the classroom, grabbed my husband's hand, and walked in ready for whatever might come as we sat down to discuss our son with the entire fourth grade teaching team.

Dressed for Battle

As Moses and the Israelites stood facing the Red Sea before them and the Egyptian Army behind them, Esther was so poised between approaching the king unsummoned or doing nothing while the Jewish death decree was enacted. This required the approximately nineteen-year-old Esther to find a courage and bravery beyond herself.

Some Jewish scholars note that on the third day, Esther "adorned royalty. It doesn't say that she wore royal garments but rather that she adorned royalty, 'alluding to the divine (Holy) Spirit."₁ In other words, they believe Esther wasn't dressed and ready for battle because of her fashion choices that day but because her three days of fasting, praying, and seeking God clothed her with the Spirit of God.

Even more intriguing is a traditional Jewish belief about what Esther prayed as she passed the pillars of the pagan court to make her request of King Ahasuerus: "Rabbi Levi said, when she passed the idols the divine spirit left her and she pleaded My G-d my G-d, why did you leave me?!"₂

Does that sound familiar?

My God, my God, why have you forsaken me?
Why are you so far from saving me,

from the words of my groaning?

Psalm 22:1

And about the ninth hour Jesus cried out with a loud voice, saying, "Eli, Eli lema sabachthani?" that is, "My God, my God, why have you forsaken me?"

Matthew 27:46

Esther. An unexpected yet appointed person to plead to a king on behalf of her people, seeking to save them from certain death.

Jesus. An unexpected Messiah anointed to plead with his blood to the King on behalf of all people to save us from a certain death.

Esther. Prepared for battle through intense prayer.

Jesus. Prepared for a battle, that he knew would cost him dearly, through intense prayer in the Garden of Gethsemane.

And so, it shall be that we best prepare ourselves for the hardest moments of life as Jesus did, through concentrated, private, and surrendered prayer.

And when you fast, do not look gloomy like the hypocrites, for they disfigure their faces that their fasting may be seen by others. Truly, I say to you, they have received their reward.

Matthew 6:16

The book of Esther presents a message about the gospel over and again as Esther and Mordecai's lives foretell the rhythms of following Jesus. Sometimes life will bring us to deep, anguished, and intense times of prayer. In these seasons, we dress for the battle by deferring distractions in order to seek God most fully. Then we march forward, clothed and ready, like Esther did.

The entirety of Esther's life reflects the spiritual formation described by Eugene Peterson in the title of his book *A Long Obedience in the Same Direction: Discipleship in an Instant Society*.3 We can see through Esther's actions that Mordecai had raised her in the traditions of their fathers, holding fast to their faith even while exiled in a pagan land. She did not suddenly summon up the courage to approach the king, but rather she acted boldly through a deep well of belief that had been nurtured throughout her life.

We, too, choose God, moment by moment, reminding ourselves with confidence that all incremental investments to growing our belief will bloom fruit for the rest of our lives—particularly in times of crisis. The seeds are planted when we carry out the instructions of the apostle Paul.

Finally, be strong in the Lord and in the strength of his might. Put on the whole armor of God, that you may be able to stand against the schemes of the devil. For we do not wrestle against flesh and blood, but against the rulers, against the authorities,

against the cosmic powers over this present darkness, against the

spiritual forces of evil in the heavenly places.

Therefore, take up the whole armor of God, that you may be able to

withstand in the evil day, and having done all, to stand firm. Stand

therefore, having fastened on the belt of truth, and having put on

the breastplate of righteousness, and, as shoes for your feet, having

put on the readiness given by the gospel of peace. In all

circumstances take up the shield of faith,

with which you can extinguish all the flaming darts of the evil

one; and take the helmet of salvation, and the sword of the Spirit,

which is the word of God, praying at all times in the Spirit, with all

prayer and supplication. To that end, keep alert with all

perseverance,

making supplication for all the saints.

Ephesians 6:10-18

Daily, and some days, moment after moment, we intentionally "dress" ourselves with God's truth, righteousness, readiness, peace, faith, salvation, the Word, and prayer. We do this in our private lives, but we are to do so in community with other believers as well.

• *Do you dress yourself for battle on a daily basis? As troubles rise, is it your reflex to turn to prayer, or to turn elsewhere?*

• *What is your biggest struggle right now? Use BibleGateway or a concordance to find a verse that resonates with you and begin to repeat that truth to yourself, arming yourself with the Word of God, described in the Ephesians passage above as the Sword.*

• With your own battles in mind, take time to read these Scriptures to preach to yourself and build faith that God fights for us in all of our battles.

- o Deuteronomy 20:1-4
- o 1 Samuel 17:45-47
- o Psalm 44:1-7
- o Proverbs 21:31
- o 2 Corinthians 2:14

Reaching for His Hem

In the last chapter, we looked at the golden scepter as a symbol of the direct access we have to the throne of God through Jesus' death. Let's consider the interaction between the king and Esther in regard to this extended scepter as Esther drew near the throne of Ahasuerus.

When the king looked to the entrance of the throne room, he saw Esther through the people and surroundings, and she won favor with him (Esther 5:2). He thus extended the scepter, granting direct access. The king made it clear that she could dare to enter to speak with him.

Yet no exchange occurred until Esther approached and reached out to touch the tip of the scepter. Esther was dealing with a proud and temperamental pagan king. She wasn't called or summoned to come to this conversation.

But we are. We are called and invited, and the golden scepter has been extended to give us access to the throne of the Almighty God. However, we must act on this. We must choose to approach and reach for the golden scepter. All too often we find excuses, avoiding such intentional effort. We have a God who sees us from his throne in heaven. Through Jesus, we've won God's favor and are summoned to come and speak with him, having direct access at all times.

Yet no change will come, no intimacy will grow, until we make the step toward him and touch the tip of the golden scepter. He is listening and ready. But are we? Are we talking? Are we taking advantage of this great privilege and regarding it as the profound freedom it is?

Esther gives us a beautiful picture of an appropriate attitude as we approach the king. She showed courage to move forward, well aware of Ahasuerus' power. She approached with humility and surrender, in the proper position of her relationship to the one who ruled. She showed tact and patience with restraint and obedience.

As she approached, Esther was fully aware of the king's track record and history when she moved and reached out toward him. This reminds me of a woman whose story is found in the New Testament.

And there was a woman who had had a discharge of blood for twelve years, and though she had spent all her living on physicians, she could not be healed by anyone. She came up behind him and touched the fringe of his garment, and immediately her discharge of blood ceased. And Jesus said, "Who was it that touched

me?" When all denied it, Peter said, "Master, the crowds surround

you and are pressing in on you!" But Jesus said, "Someone

touched me, for I perceive that power has gone out from me." And

when the woman saw that she was not hidden, she came trembling,

and falling down before him declared in the presence of all the

people why she had touched him, and how she had been

immediately healed. And he said to her, "Daughter, your faith has

made you well; go in peace."

Luke 8:43-48

This woman in Luke simply reached for the hem of Jesus. Humble

yet bold, she, like Esther, chose to make the move and reach out to

touch the one whose reputation proceeded him. In stark contrast to

Ahasuerus, our faithful Eternal King is unmatched in his

lovingkindness. His goodness and grace and love are unsearchable.

His faithfulness is unending. When threats come against our very life, our family, our future, our emotions, we can stop and pause at the throne of God. We can bring to mind his track record, recalling

how he's shown up before to remind our doubts that he will show up again. We boldly move toward the King and let our requests be made known. We reach for his hem day after day, confident of his love and faithfulness toward us.

Bring these images to mind as you find time for such a habit. Humble yourself in awe and take full advantage of the great privilege of prayer that's been extended to you. As you wait for the answers, which you often will, do not give up. Instead, be like the persistent widow in Luke 18:1, knowing that "we ought always to pray and to not give up."

Responding to Opposition

Within Esther 5, we see three people respond to opposition in very different ways. Becoming a student of these responses can offer great instruction for our own difficult situations.

1—*Prayerful and Humbled (Esther)*

Fighting off her initial fears and even the comfort of her current position within the palace, Esther chose to act. However, she wouldn't humble herself before her husband to make supplication until she'd humbled herself before her God to do the same. Furthermore, she asks her fellow Jews and handmaidens to join in the petition, seeking community and corporate prayer.

It is the incubator of great courage and discernment when we join together with others and seek the Lord wholeheartedly. Surely, it was this prayerful preparation that would later inform Esther to defer her ultimate request until she twice served the king and Haman a feast. Though the king offered "up to half of his kingdom" (which was a proverbial offer and not literal), 4 she asks him to dinner rather than asking him to save her people.

Not only that, but she asks him to bring Haman along as well.

Esther dealt with the evil and vengeful man behind the dark threat by inviting him to a feast, likely of wine and fruit according to Persian customs. 5 Commentators vary as to the reasoning behind her polite invitation and the initial deferment of the big ask. Was she daunted by the task? Was she keeping her enemy close, intending to reveal the villain with him present? Was she garnering favor with the king by including his top official? Was it a lack of courage that led Esther to extend the invitation for a second banquet? And, what I want to know, what on earth was the dinner conversation like?

All that we know for certain is that Esther sought the Lord on the matter and proceeded with divine direction. We, too, can be assured that he will lead us forward as we keep seeking, whether our actions make sense or not. We listen carefully to the nudges and learn to trust them as Spirit-led prompting. As we do so, we grow in our fluency with such nudges and our willingness to obey.

This picture of inviting others to a feast is a picture of living for Jesus. We've been invited to feast with the King so we can invite others to feast. Loved people love others. Welcomed people welcome others. We have been shown the goodness of God by the grace that transformed us from an enemy of God to a child of God. Because of this, we can show goodness, even to our enemy, with a humility and gentleness born of a firm understanding of grace. Surrendered people can trust God when he asks us to show good to those who haven't earned it.

You prepare a table before me

in the presence of my enemies;

you anoint my head with oil;

my cup overflows.

Surely goodness and mercy shall follow me

all the days of my life,

and I shall dwell in the house of the Lord

forever.

Psalm 23:5-6

2—Unflinching (Mordecai)

Throughout the book of Esther, Mordecai remained resolute. He faithfully raised his orphaned cousin, seemingly all on his own, and he was faithful in his presence at the king's gate. He worked and paced there for a year waiting on word of Esther. Then, he continued to stand there, declining to bow to Haman. Unyielding in his mourning, he refused to remove his sackcloth, and he was certain in his assertion that Esther must risk the death sentence and approach the king to plead for their people.

Mordecai dealt with opposition as he seemed to approach life. One day at a time, he kept on keeping on. There at the gate, he continued to refuse Haman the worship so desired. Even while his beloved cousin took the risk that he had requested of her, Mordecai went to work and neither trembled nor showed fear as Haman passed by, as if it were an ordinary day. A humbled man steadfast in faith can dare to avoid concern with the opinion, whims, or plots of other people.

My dad was like this. He obeyed and loved and served, seemingly undisturbed by life in general. The first time I really saw him cry was when I was seventeen years old and there was the suspicion of a second cancer occurrence. Yet, when told in recovery that the surgery was unsuccessful and the cancer had fatally spread, he replied firmly, "For to me, to live is Christ, and to die is gain" (Philippians 1:21).

And so, it was. It was the way he lived until he died. Only as an adult, have I grasped the deep trust my father must have had in his heavenly Father. His childhood included tragedy and hardship. In college, during an unpopular war, he chose ROTC and planned to volunteer to join the Army. He served for a year in the Vietnam War, training the Vietnamese to fight the communists. When his first born was a baby, he went back for another year to serve in combat. There, during a landmine explosion, Dad was injured. After six weeks of recovering in Japan, he went right back to combat.

My dad was like Mordecai. He ultimately dealt with the plot twists of life by running to God. He could humble himself before the circumstances that opposed him because he stayed humbled before the One who changed him.

3 – Reactive (Haman)

Letting your emotions lead your decisions and actions is a dangerous way to live. More often than not, your reactions take control of you. Fear, pride, and materialism are liars and bullies.

Obviously, Haman was not genuinely "joyful and glad of heart" as described in Esther 5:9. We quickly see his volatility swinging wildly from one emotional extreme to another. We observe him unraveled with rage because one man, Mordecai, denied him. Why he expected anything different at this point of the narrative is puzzling as Haman had already exacted his revenge for such behavior through the death sentence for all Jews.

Therein lies the problem with emotions. They are so unpredictable, toppling like a house of cards with the slightest breeze. The problem with a self-worth and a happiness built on the applause of man is that it cannot endure as a solid foundation. The fragility of flattery is that it torments the proud to madness when it isn't offered as expected.

Haman himself uttered the best commentary on the idea of building your life on earthly riches, status, and approval when he declared at the end of Esther 5 that these things didn't satisfy. Though wealthy, with ten sons, promotions, status, and an invitation to dine a second time with the queen and king, Haman stated, "all this is worth nothing to me" because one Jewish man who had never shown him honor continued to do just that.

Though Mordecai was a dead man walking, Haman found solace only in a plan for an immediate and humiliating death. It's an illogical way to deal with this particular opposition. But then again, hatred and vanity rarely listen to logic.

Needing Truth-Speakers

As Haman bemoaned his situation, the idea of building the gallows was the brainchild of the counsel with which he surrounded himself. They suggested he build a seventy-five-foot pole with a pointed tip, literally advising a plan that was overkill. This type of execution involved spearing the victim at the top, then pulling him down by the legs until he was impaled for a slow death. Haman's wife and all of his friends were reacting in kind to Haman's hatred. They were stroking his ego rather than reminding him that not only Mordecai, but all the Jews would be destroyed within a few months.

This demonstrates the nature of sin even as it was born into the world. The serpent destroyed the purity and perfection of the garden by telling Eve what she wanted to hear. He spoke to her vanity and her own gain. One of the most perilous positions we can create in our lives is to surround ourselves with ego-builders rather than truth-speakers.

We've all been there. As middle school girls, we asked our friends if we looked okay, wanting them to say only what we wanted to hear. We've also been on the flipside, saying what we know was expected in order to move the conversation along or to appease those around us.

The deceit of popularity is that it's a moving target. The lure of the "in-crowd" seduces a following who are chained to the impulses of trend. Even Haman, in the company of his own crowd, admitted it's never enough. We are made with eternity set in our hearts by our Creator. As long as we deny that space the proper satisfaction, it will never find its worth.

While uncomfortable and difficult, we must be courageous enough to intentionally seek a community of truth-speakers. We don't need counsel that will respond to our admitted emptiness by fueling our fickle feelings. We need counsel that will call out the sin of empty pursuits. We need to cultivate friendships that will dare to love us enough to say that envy, vanity, and hatred are actually tormenting us.

It takes a heart secure in the grace of God and hungry for his glory to be bold enough to want such company. It takes a vulnerability and a soul-deep desire for authenticity as well as a bravery that reminds itself that truth brings freedom.

In my own life, it took a three-year battle with depression and anxiety to break me free of the chains of some positions and places that were ego-builders. When things got tough, the road got lonely. Truly, God was ordaining the path through the desert, and, like the Israelites leaving Egypt, I took plunder with me as I was set free from the captivity of ego-building.

The sudden void of these things brought the slow realization of how unsatisfying they were. I found that more time with God and in his Word brought a greater hunger for it. I hardly realized it was happening, but the remarkable riches of the entire experience was

204

finding the fulfillment of truth-speakers. I have to be intentional to stay in touch with them, and I have to return the favor, humbled enough to be surrendered to the work of sanctification.

Response to Esther 5

The Word of God is meant to transform and call us to action. Take some time to consider the questions below and write out your responses.

• *Stop and think about your relationship with God. How can you become more intentional to reach for the hem of Jesus and grow in intimacy with him?*

• *In dealing with opposition, are you most like Esther, Mordecai, or Haman, and why?*

• *Considering your closest confidants, do you lean more toward seeking ego-builders or truth-speakers? Which one do you tend to be for those closest to you?*

• *Who is one person who "spurs you toward good deeds" (Hebrews 10:24), and faithfully turns you back to God's truth? How might you cultivate that friendship and return the favor?*

• *Are you actively involved in a church small group or Bible study that is a tribe of truth-speakers? If not, are you willing to change this?*

The Truths of Esther 5

Let's wrap up this section of Scripture by considering these three elements.

1—Adoration of God from Esther 5

- You are the God who sees me.
- You are the God who extended the golden scepter of your own Son, Jesus, to give me direct access to you.
- You are the God who sits enthroned over the entire universe.
- You are the God who clothes me in your royal robes of righteousness.
- You are the God who equips me for battle.
- You are the God who rules and reigns over the enemy.
- You are the God who hears my pleas.
- You are the God who is accessible and approachable.
- You are the God who prepares a table before me in the presence of my enemies.
- You are the God who alone is worthy of worship.

- You are the God whose truth sets me free and who calls me to walk in it.

2—Affirmation of Our Gospel Identity from Esther 5

- I am clothed in salvation.

- I am welcomed and invited to approach the throne of grace with confidence.

- I am seen and heard and have God's favor because of Jesus.

- I am invited in so that I can invite and serve others.

- I am loved in order to love others.

- I am freed in order to free others.

- I am held by grace and understanding that equips me to extend it to others.

3—Actions to Take from Esther 5

- I am to approach and reach for Jesus with all my concerns, every day.

- I am to pray and fast privately, not for appearance sake.

- I am to build belief through daily habits of seeking God.

- I am to serve others humbly.

- I am called to gentleness and patience.

- I am not to demand attention or approval.

- I am to rest in God's favor and not the favor of men.

- I am to keep on faithfully and steadfastly.

- I am to bow to God alone.

- I am to guard against discontent, pride, and being led by emotions.

- I am to be a truth-speaker and to have truth-speakers in my life.

- I am not to seek or demand the posturing of others.

- I am to remember how man's praise and status are never satisfying.

Conclusion of Esther 5

Life includes battles, both big and small. These range from the daily battles for our time and attention that dictate our affections to the battles of health problems, relationship issues, job losses, and other such trials. The composition of our character for the big battles is determined by our response to the smaller ones. We can look around us, which can lead to comparison and dissatisfaction, or we can keep our sights on God, cheered on by the truth-speakers with whom we intentionally surround ourselves.

ESTHER 6

And Haman said to himself, "Whom would the king

delight to honor more than me?"

Esther 6:6

Esther 6, *English Standard Version*

The King Honors Mordecai

6 On that night the king could not sleep. And he gave orders to bring the book of memorable deeds, the chronicles, and they were read before the king. 2 And it was found written how Mordecai had told about Bigthana and Teresh, two of the king's eunuchs, who guarded the threshold, and who had sought to lay hands on King Ahasuerus. 3 And the king said, "What honor or distinction has been bestowed on Mordecai for this?" The king's young men who attended him said, "Nothing has been done for him." 4 And the king said, "Who is in the court?" Now Haman had just entered the outer court of the king's palace to speak to the king about having Mordecai hanged on the gallows that he had prepared for him.5 And the king's young men told him, "Haman is there, standing in the court." And the king said, "Let him come in." 6 So Haman came in, and the king said to him, "What should be done to the man whom the king delights to honor?" And Haman said to himself, "Whom would the king delight to honor more than me?" 7 And Haman said to the king, "For the man whom the king delights to honor, 8 let royal robes be

brought, which the king has worn, and the horse that the king has ridden, and on whose head a royal crown is set. 9 And let the robes and the horse be handed over to one of the king's most noble officials. Let them dress the man whom the king delights to honor, and let them lead him on the horse through the square of the city, proclaiming before him: 'Thus shall it be done to the man whom the king delights to honor.'" 10 Then the king said to Haman, "Hurry; take the robes and the horse, as you have said, and do so to Mordecai the Jew, who sits at the king's gate. Leave out nothing that you have mentioned." 11 So Haman took the robes and the horse, and he dressed Mordecai and led him through the square of the city, proclaiming before him, "Thus shall it be done to the man whom the king delights to honor."

12 Then Mordecai returned to the king's gate. But Haman hurried to his house, mourning and with his head covered. 13 And Haman told his wife Zeresh and all his friends everything that had happened to him. Then his wise men and his wife Zeresh said to him, "If Mordecai, before whom you have begun to fall, is of the Jewish people, you will not overcome him but will surely fall before him."

Esther Reveals Haman's Plot

14 While they were yet talking with him, the king's eunuchs arrived and hurried to bring Haman to the feast that Esther had prepared.

A GOD WE CAN TRUST

Esther 6

When Chris and I realized we were outgrowing our first house, we began to pray about the next steps. Our journey to find our current home is one of faith, where detail after detail lined up in a way that can only be attributed to divine providence. It's one of our favorite God stories to tell.

We had received a great offer on our house but hadn't found a home to purchase within the same area. The next day, my oldest son needed something at the store. On a whim, I decided to drive down a street to check out a house that had suddenly disappeared from the MLS website. We turned the corner, and as we approached the intended home, a man stood in the yard of the home next to it. He was pushing a "For Sale by Owner" sign into the yard.

Without thinking, I put on the brakes and backed up. I rolled down my window and asked if I was his first customer. Such boldness is usually my husband's role; I'm far more the introvert. The homeowner laughed nervously, but I pushed on. I told him that I wasn't joking; we'd just gotten an offer on our house and needed to find a new one. I added that we'd always admired the quiet street, and I was seriously interested in seeing their home. About that time, his wife walked up from her vantage point in the garage.

When I asked for details about the house, they affirmed each thing we'd wanted. I was not going to be deterred, and, surprising myself, I requested to see the house. They were on their way to dinner so I boldly asked if we could come after that. I'm sure at this point, they were quite leery of me, but they saw my son in the car and agreed reluctantly.

I had a feeling about it as I drove home, but was disappointed when we couldn't line up a babysitter. We gave our kids, then ages 3, 7, and 9, stern warnings about behaving well, and marched on in. From the minute I stepped into the foyer, it felt like home. What I learned that night is that the couple were the original homeowners who had raised their children there. The husband was ready for his retirement home on a lake, but the wife was hesitant. He'd convinced her to just throw out a sign in the yard to see what happened.

She obviously was ill-prepared for a pushy stranger to barge in a few hours later. Yet she was drawn to my children. The mother in her was able to see the future of her beloved home where another couple could raise their own children.

Who, but God?

Every day of our lives, our big God is at work in details we can't even comprehend, weaving each step of our journey for his glory. We just need eyes to see and take note, and then to rehearse this history whenever doubt creeps in.

Weaver of All Details

The second chapter of Esther ended with a sudden interruption to the narrative about Esther. Seemingly misplaced, there's the account of

Mordecai uncovering an assassination plot, which was reported to the king and investigated after Mordecai informed Esther. The villains were killed, and life went on.

While we know that Esther was named queen in the seventh year of King Ahasuerus' reign and the death decree for Jews was issued in the twelfth year of his reign, we don't know the exact timing between the uncovered assassination plot and the beginning of Esther 6. We can safely assume several years have passed, bringing a great pause since the actions of Mordecai were noted in the king's book of annals.

Few of us do well with such pauses in life. Within us is a desire for instant gratification, exacerbated by our current culture. Waiting for anything is difficult—particularly waiting on God. For everyone in a season of wondering how it all works together and when relief will come, whether it be a major life interruption or just a tedious sameness in life, be encouraged by the truths we find within Esther 6.

The miracle of God's Sovereignty is far beyond our comprehension, particularly when bad things happen. The heart of any crisis of faith is whether you can choose to believe that God is still good and can weave a kingdom purpose from that which feels senseless.

The heart of man plans his way,

but the LORD establishes his steps.

Proverbs 16:9

Many are the plans in the mind of a man,

but it is the purpose of the LORD that will stand.

Proverbs 19:21

To instruct your choice about what to believe, consider how Mordecai's story unfolds. After the pause between Esther 2 and Esther 6, one night the king "happened" to be unable to sleep. He who ruled over a vast empire couldn't control his sleep habits. He could have called for any distraction or entertainment that his heart desired. Yet he gave orders for the book of memorable deeds to be read.

The original Hebrew root word for "read" means to be called, to be summoned, announce, proclaim. I The king who couldn't be approached without being summoned, now summoned for a book to be read. Of all the books, of all the pages, the king's personal attendants turned to the account of Mordecai saving the king. In an unusual move for this temperamental pagan king, he showed consideration for a common man when he asked how the man had been honored.

Right then, at that exact moment, as the king was ruminating on this, Haman appeared in the outer court. At what would seem an unlikely hour, Haman sought an audience with the king because he couldn't put his anger to rest. Haman, inflamed by hatred and pride, assumed that he alone would be the one the king would delight to honor when the king brought up the matter.

220

But God.

The One who knits us in our mother's womb is indeed weaving our stories together, though sometimes the progress and end result remain unclear. We see only what's in front of us, so we must remember that it is but a shadow of the eternal.

In God's timing, he used Haman's own suggestions to mastermind the way for Haman's archnemesis Mordecai to be honored. Though it seemed the thwarted assassination plot had long been forgotten, God had never lost sight of it. He used the daily places of Mordecai's work for the purpose of Ahasuerus' kingdom, and, more importantly, he was divinely using it all for his eternal kingdom.

Your eyes saw my unformed substance;

in your book were written,

every one of them,

the days that were formed for me,

when as yet

there was none of them.

Psalm 139:16

When you are in a season of questioning purpose and timing for your life, be assured, there is a book of remembrance. All your days were written before one came to be by a God who, unbound by time, sees our past, present, and future. He is the King who takes notice of us, and he will, in his divine providence, work all things together, in his timing, for our eternal good and for his eternal glory when we surrender to him. Even when we can't see it or feel it or sense it, God is at work in our lives. It's simply the heart of our Abba Father for his children.

Since ancient times no one has heard,

no ear has perceived, no eye has seen any God besides you,

who acts on behalf of those who wait for him.

Isaiah 64:4 (NIV)

A King Who Delights in Us

The king who had toasted with Haman after the death decree while many were bewildered suddenly proved to have a heart to honor a lowly gatekeeper. Five times within Esther 6, we see the phrase "the man whom the king delights to honor."[2] The fact that an imperfect, pagan king is moved to kindness toward his subject offers the smallest glimpse of the lovingkindness of God.

How much more so does the King of all Kings delight to show his goodness to us? That he, the perfect Father God of all creation, would dare to send his own Son to make us his children? What higher honor can we receive than the forgiveness of sins, salvation from eternal separation from God, and to be loved so lavishly that we are called his children (1 John 3:1, NIV).

When Mordecai was honored, he was given royal robes, placed on a horse bearing the royal crest, and announced throughout the city as the man whom the king delighted to honor. This was an honor similar to that which Pharaoh granted to Joseph upon naming him second in command of Egypt in Genesis 41:43, as well as how David honored his son Solomon in 1 Kings 1:33. This was, indeed, a great honor among ancient kingdoms.

For us, Scripture outlines the honor we receive as followers of Jesus and informs us that we, too, are clothed by the King. This scene in the Garden of Eden foretells God's greater plan to cover our sins and our shame, once and for all, as he declares us objects of his delight.

And the LORD God made for Adam and for his wife garments of

skins and clothed them.

Genesis 3:21

Further insight about how our King clothes us is offered by the prophet Isaiah when he describes God's royal robes of salvation that are eternally ours when we surrender ourselves to following Jesus.

I will greatly rejoice in the LORD;

my soul shall exult in my God,

for he has clothed me with the garments of salvation;

he has covered me with the robe of righteousness,

as a bridegroom decks himself like a priest with a beautiful

headdress,

and as a bride adorns herself with her jewels.

Isaiah 61:10

The King of Kings shows generous love for us, daring to share even his royalty, as his beloved children and heirs of salvation. Because the crown of thorns was placed on the head of our Savior, we have received the crown of righteousness (2 Timothy 4:8), the crown of life (James 1:12), and the unfading crown of glory (1 Peter 5:4). There is no greater honor than to be the recipients of such extravagant grace by the Almighty God.

• Do you find delight in God? Do you sense his delight in you? If not, begin to ask him to help you feel his delight and to be humbled by gratitude for how he honors you through his love and care.

He Exalts the Humble and Humbles the Proud

When it comes to life choices, we see a study in contrast between Haman and Mordecai throughout Esther. Esther 5 ends with Haman having the gallows made. The original Hebrew word for "made" referring to the gallows is the exact word that King Ahasuerus uses when he asks what has "been done" for the man, Mordecai, who uncovered the assassination plot. [3]

Haman had the gallows built, fueled by pride and ambition.

Mordecai had an honor granted, in the midst of humble service.

As God divinely uses our daily places for his kingdom in his timing, we are to live in faithful obedience, leaving the results to God. God promises that he will exalt the humble and humble the proud. Haman's assumption that there was no one else besides himself that the king would rather honor reveals the depths of his arrogance. While he had been promoted by the king to a high position, Haman was blind to how anyone else could deserve prestige or status.

• *Where do you give yourself too much credit? Is there an area in your life where you feel that God owes you something or a blind spot where you struggle with wanting to see someone "pay" for their offense to you?*

Haman demanded honor. He thrived on applause. He was driven by ego, failing to see that his pride set a trap not for his enemy, but for himself. With the turn of the tide toward honor for Mordecai, God was revealing how he would preserve his chosen people the Israelites, giving both Haman and Mordecai what their lives had earned.

The humble and faithful Mordecai was exalted as he was paraded around town by the wicked Haman. Haman was forced to announce to all in Susa that Mordecai was honored by the king. What each of these men did next further reveals their truest character.

Unaffected by the accolades, Mordecai went back to the very spot where we have seen him over and again through the entire book of Esther. He sat at the king's gate, continuing to serve humbly and faithfully. He didn't think more of himself even after he saw Haman humiliated by the king's orders.

This Mordecai points to another humble man named Mordecai who lived in more modern times. Both the biblical Mordecai and the man known as Mordecai Ham lived quiet and faithful lives. While neither is particularly celebrated, both played an integral role in the eternal kingdom of God. You see, Mordecai Ham is the evangelist who preached at a 1934 revival where a young man saw his need for a Savior. That young man's name was Billy Graham.

Contrary to this kind of meek steadfastness, Esther 6:12 tells us that Haman hurried home in mourning, with his head covered. In the context of ancient traditions, Haman was responding as one would to the death of a very close loved one.4 His pride was indeed dealt a deadly blow when he was shamed by the king's honor for the man he despised. The shifting sand of man's opinion caused Haman to grieve profoundly because he lived and died by such approval.

Every day we can choose what to do with our lives. We can live for the applause of man, or we can live for the applause in heaven. We can see only right before us, or we can live for an eternal kingdom.

We can try to build lofty and noteworthy things with our lives, or we can choose to serve at the gate, sitting with the tedious daily tasks assigned to us.

We can be like Haman, craving status to the point that its absence devastates us. Or we can be like Mordecai, recognizing the emptiness of man's fleeting praise and building our lives for the God who never changes.

Tripped Up by Pride

As previously noted, Haman surrounded himself with ego-builders. Their poor advice from the previous chapter takes a sharp U-turn at the end of the sixth chapter of Esther. In his shame and disgrace, Haman hurried home again to Zeresh and his friends to recount what had then transpired. These "allies" now clearly saw Haman's impending doom, and, in an about-face, they suddenly predicted his downfall.

This is the problem with ego-builders. As Matthew Henry notes, "Miserable comforters are they all; they did not advise Haman to repent but foretold his fate as unavoidable." 5 While just a few verses back they advised Haman to take extreme measures against Mordecai, they now callously offer no support.

His advisors and his wife Zeresh said to him, "Since Mordecai before whom your downfall has started, is of Jewish origin, you cannot stand against him—you will surely come to ruin!"

Esther 6:13 (NIV)

The NIV translation offers a fascinating connection. The verbiage "surely come to ruin" used here in verse 13 comes from the Hebrew "napal," which means to "fall, fail, to cause to fall, to drop, to cast down, to fall prostrate (to worship), to fall upon (to attack), and it is used of casting lots." 6 Indeed, this is the exact word used in Esther 3:7 when the king cast (*napal*) the Pur, or the lot, in the presence of Haman to select the day for the destruction of the Jews.

When we live for the temporal and fleeting, we are rolling the dice. Matthew 6 expresses that we are receiving our reward in full if we live to perform for others and to be applauded. Things may seem to be going in our favor, but they quickly can become our ruin.

He will render to each one according to his works:
to those who by patience in well-doing seek for glory and honor
and immortality, he will give eternal life;
but for those who are self-seeking and do not obey the truth, but
obey unrighteousness, there will be wrath and fury.
Romans 2:6-8

So we do not lose heart. Though our outer self is wasting away,
our inner self is being renewed day by day.
For this light momentary affliction is preparing for us
an eternal weight of glory beyond all comparison,

as we look not to the things that are seen but to the things that are

unseen. For the things that are seen are transient, but the things

that are unseen are eternal.

2 Corinthians 4:16-18

Undoubtedly, from beginning to end, this chapter of Esther reveals that our God is the God of details. He is the one who orders our lives and secures our eternity. He is the one whose everlasting kingdom will stand, no matter what battles seem to be lost along the way.

Response to Esther 6

The Word of God is meant to transform and call us to action. Take some time to consider the questions below and write out your responses.

• *What details of your life are you having trouble understanding? What intentional things can you do to help you build belief and faith in God as trustworthy with these details?*

• *If absolute acceptance and delight is not your default on how God feels toward you, then begin to pray regularly that he might heal your unbelief.*

• *Can you be content living an anonymous life, faithfully serving the Lord with humility, even if no one ever notices it?*

• *Where can you acknowledge areas of pride that may be tripping you up in your pursuit of Christ?*

• In your life, where are you "rolling the dice" for temporal gain and where are you increasingly chasing the eternal?

• Do you rely on a community of ego-builders or of truth-speakers with the common goal of building Jesus' name and not your own?

The Truths of Esther 6

Let's wrap up this section of Scripture by considering these three elements.

1—Adoration of God from Esther 6

- You are the God who can work all the details of our lives for our eternal good and your glory.
- You are the God who is divine providence and sovereign.

- You are the God who knows all our days and all our times.

- You are the God who holds us through all our days.

- You are the God who is the king who sees me.

- You are the God who delights in your children.

- You are the God who clothes us with salvation, though we are undeserving of such honor.

- You are the God who is caring, loving, and just.

- You are the God who is judge and protector.

- You are the God who is trustworthy.

- You are the God whose purposes will not fail.

2—Affirmation of Our Gospel Identity from Esther 6

- I am held firmly in God's divine purposes.

- I am a servant who is accepted by my King.

- I am cared for in every detail and God's perfect timing.

- I am a source of delight to my King.

- I am a child of God who can trust him to defend my cause.

3—Actions to Take from Esther 6

- I am to trust all my times to his hands.

- I am to stand firm and keep serving him, no matter if anyone notices.

- I am to avoid being prideful or living for the applause of man.

- I am to serve humbly and faithfully.

- I am not to be puffed up by any accolade granted.

- I am to avoid revenge, pride, and hatred.

- I am to not think of myself as above any calling or purpose of God.

- I am to be wary of ego-builders in my own life.

- I am to surrender my day to God, allowing him to order my steps.

Conclusion of Esther 6

In "whatever we do, we work heartily for the Lord and not man" (Colossians 3:23). With our eyes locked on the kingdom to come, we can look beyond the temporal. We must rehearse and remember God's goodness and delight in us in order to continually build to the point of surrendering all of our work, all of our days, and all of the results to his eternal purposes.

This is the foundation on which we can establish a trust that says whether I'm noticed or not, I know my King is for me. Whether things are going poorly or well, I will humble myself to his sovereignty.

It's counterintuitive to live for the unseen and the yet to come rather than status, approval, and temporal gain. Yet Jesus showed us how to live for such an upside-down kingdom. He, the Son of God, became an enemy bearing our sins, so that we, enemies of God, could become sons and daughters of God. Thus, we follow in the footsteps of the Son of God by setting our gaze on our Father and choosing humbled obedience to him.

ESTHER 7

Then, the wrath of the king abated.

Esther 7:10b

Esther 7, *English Standard Version*

7 So the king and Haman went in to feast with Queen Esther. 2 And on the second day, as they were drinking wine after the feast, the king again said to Esther, "What is your wish, Queen Esther? It shall be granted you. And what is your request? Even to the half of my kingdom, it shall be fulfilled." 3 Then Queen Esther answered, "If I have found favor in your sight, O king, and if it please the king, let my life be granted me for my wish, and my people for my request. 4 For we have been sold, I and my people, to be destroyed, to be killed, and to be annihilated. If we had been sold merely as slaves, men and women, I would have been silent, for our affliction is not to be compared with the loss to the king." 5 Then King Ahasuerus said to Queen Esther, "Who is he, and where is he, who has dared to do this?" 6 And Esther said, "A foe and enemy! This wicked Haman!" Then Haman was terrified before the king and the queen.

Haman Is Hanged

7 And the king arose in his wrath from the wine-drinking and went into the palace garden, but Haman stayed to beg for his life from Queen Esther, for he saw that harm was determined against him by

the king. 8 And the king returned from the palace garden to the place where they were drinking wine, as Haman was falling on the couch where Esther was. And the king said, "Will he even assault the queen in my presence, in my own house?" As the word left the mouth of the king, they covered Haman's face. 9 Then Harbona, one of the eunuchs in attendance on the king, said, "Moreover, the gallows that Haman has prepared for Mordecai, whose word saved the king, is standing at Haman's house, fifty cubits high." And the king said, "Hang him on that." 10 So they hanged Haman on the gallows that he had prepared for Mordecai. Then the wrath of the king abated.

A TASTE OF GRACE
Esther 7

When I looked at my phone and saw my son's name, just moments after he left the house, I knew something was wrong. His voice was remarkably calm as he said, "Mom, I got in a wreck. I'm okay, but the car is totaled and so is the other car." With my heart flipping cartwheels, I tried to ask the right questions about his location and calling the police before I headed his way.

I gave my daughter a quick explanation and hurriedly called my husband while climbing into my van. Despite Collin's reassurances of his welfare, my mind suddenly went blank. Main Street. How do I get to Main Street? Considering that we've lived in the same area for over twenty years, my mental fog revealed how rattled I was.

I prayed as I drove, having to redirect as I got lost on the short drive to Main Street. Nothing had prepared me for what I saw when I pulled to the intersection. I was looking at the underside of a Jeep® Cherokee, now resting on the driver's side, next to a large light pole.

Police cars, fire trucks, and ambulances surrounded the scene in a whirl of flashing lights. Straight ahead, I could see my son standing in the middle of first responders, with his car nearby, crushed on the passenger side.

Reason seldom has a voice in the midst of panic. Although I could see he was okay, my thoughts swirled about who was in the flipped car and what Collin had seen and experienced. I threw my van in park and ran to Collin, who was surprisingly composed. I gave him the glance over, seeing no blood or injury, while a policeman tried to tell me what happened and then reported, "The other driver is fine. She was alone in the vehicle and isn't injured."

When Collin later recounted the details, the miracle of the situation became clearer. He was driving straight through an intersection at a green light and told me, "Mom, these cars were turning left in front of me, gunning it through the intersection. When I saw that Jeep®, I knew I couldn't avoid it. So, I thought to brake and turn my passenger side to it, maybe just clipping it there for the least impact."

After the airbags deployed and his car came to a stop, he threw it in park and ran to try to help the other driver who was, by then, crouching on the driver's side window, then flush to the ground. While dialing 911, three men came and tried to get the woman out. Afraid to tip the car or cause more harm, they decided to wait for the first responders who rescued her by breaking out the rear window and directing her to crawl to the back.

When I arrived just moments after the wreck, there were no witnesses. No one was there to offer a statement about trying to rescue the woman. Where these three men came from was a mystery to me as it is not an intersection where pedestrians would be. The firefighter who helped me take everything out of Collin's car stopped me and said that my son handled this situation better than most adults would have.

Looking at the photos, I realized the magnitude of what could have happened. Those cars came to rest right next to a pole, but they didn't hit it. I believe only God could have equipped my seventeen-year-old to know how to respond in the five seconds he had to brace for impact. Somehow, three mystery men appeared from nowhere to calm both drivers and offer assistance.

The fact that God so mercifully spared my son hit me hard. He preserved Collin's life and protected the other driver. He, who did not spare his own Son for our sakes, chose to divinely reach in at that moment and spare my son. God was giving a clear picture of the grace that I have always struggled to understand at a soul level. The chains of a faith built on performance were loosed that day. The reality of grace was displayed against the backdrop of a situation where I could have lost what God so willingly chose himself to sacrifice.

The Promise to Come

It's humbling to admit that this lifelong church girl never realized that every single story in the Bible is a picture of the promises fulfilled through Jesus. Although I had been taught about the "scarlet thread" throughout Scripture, foreshadowing the coming Messiah, it has only been in the last five years that I've begun to truly understand the gospel story.

My journey has included difficult demolitions of a works mentality and a faith propped up by self-righteousness. Letting go of any need to prove myself and embracing my status as a sinner has ushered in a great awakening to grace, equipping me to more fully experience the wonder of the gospel. When we overlay the gospel to the seventh chapter of Esther, fresh amazement is stirred at the miracle we've been given through Jesus.

Our Role in the Gospel

The story of each of us can be found within all three central figures in this chapter of Esther.

First, we can see ourselves in Esther.

In our status as a slave to sin and an exile from the kingdom of God, doomed to certain death, we are undeserving to offer any plea or to be heard. However, our King audaciously gives us an audience with him. This grace provides the privilege of intercession, not just for our own lives, but also for the lives of others.

• *Consider how often you plead with the Father for the salvation and well-being of others, acting as Esther did with her daring petition. Who might you more fervently petition for before the Father?*

In the opening verses of chapter 7, Esther again exemplifies how to petition the king, with a humble and surrendered posture, remembering her standing as one unqualified to make demands of the ruler. She repeatedly used the word "if," as in if I have found favor, and if the king is pleased. There before him a second time, she also found the courage to ask for her life and the lives of her people, going on to boldly expose the evil plots against her by the very man that the king had previously promoted.

Secondly, the actions of King Ahasuerus also reflect our position within the bigger gospel story.

When Esther finally revealed Haman's plot, the king naively questioned her about who would be so conniving to create such a vile plan. He had been so deceived by Haman that he was oblivious to his own contribution and role in the scheme.

Judge not, that you be not judged. For with the judgment you pronounce you will be judged, and with the measure you use it will be measured to you. Why do you see the speck that is in your brother's eye, but do not notice the log that is in your own eye? Or how can you say to your brother, 'Let me take the speck out of your eye,' when there is the log in your own eye? You hypocrite first take the log out of your own eye, and then you will see clearly to take the speck out of your brother's eye.

Matthew 7:1-5

⟶ - ⟵

Ahasuerus, so enraged by the speck in the eye of the one who devised such destruction, didn't see the log in his own (Matthew 7:4). Mothering has taught me that the very things that I find exasperating in my children's behavior are often a reflection of my own habits. Rather than pointing to those around us, we must be willing to move past our self-deceptions to evaluate our own need for transformation, asking God continually for wisdom to see and courage to confront our own areas of sin and weakness.

• *Is there a blind spot in your own life where you tend to ignore a sin habit or pattern? What is it?*

Thirdly, the hard reality is that we can also find ourselves in the person of Haman within this chapter.

And Esther said, "A foe and an enemy! This wicked Haman!"

Then Haman was terrified before the king and the queen.

Esther 7:6

Pride will keep us from being awed by the grace of God because it lies to us about our desperate need for it. We, too, are wicked and vile, an enemy, and unable to earn our own salvation. In fact, the Hebrew root word for "wicked" within the verse above is the same word used in Genesis 2:9 and 3:4 when describing the tree of the knowledge of good and evil in the garden. [1]

Like Haman's covered face when he is condemned to die, we continually try to hide our sins punishable by death, acting like Adam and Eve when they shielded themselves with leaves in the presence of God. We are often unwilling to let our wickedness be exposed, even to ourselves.

God's Grace

God is the king who sits enthroned above the earth. His reign has no beginning and no end. Though sovereign and holy, he invites us to interact with him, listening and speaking to us. He delights to show us mercy while fully aware of our struggles and hardships. Though he knows our failures and sins, he desires that we grow in an intimate relationship with him. This requires that we agree with him in confession regarding our sins thereby falling absolutely on the grace he offers.

We grow in our awe at and belief in the gospel of grace only when we are able to continually release ourselves of any entitlement to what God's grace gives. When we grow in confidence that we can never earn a seat at the table, then we most fully embrace the generosity of God, poised perfectly to serve and live with extravagant generosity toward others.

The Cost of Grace

The close of Esther 7 illustrates the only reason that we are afforded kindness from the Almighty God. We, sinful and broken, can never be saved by pleading for our lives before the throne through our own merit. The intolerable weight of the sins of the world required that Someone hang on a pole and die a brutal and public death to give us such standing, as Ahasuerus required the death of Haman on the wooden pole before his anger was abated.

So they hanged Haman on the gallows that he had prepared for

Mordecai. Then the wrath of the king abated.

Esther 7:10

The Enemy

Haman sought to destroy, kill, and annihilate the people of God within the entire kingdom of Ahasuerus. We, too, have an enemy who seeks to "kill, steal, and destroy" (John 10:10). While Haman seemingly enjoyed comfort, wealth, and status for a time, his pride ensured his ultimate downfall. His true intentions were laid bare before King Ahasuerus with the realization that the benefit of the kingdom was never Haman's priority but rather building a kingdom for himself. This ambition had driven Haman to have the public spectacle of a 75-foot pole constructed on which to impale the one person whose only offense was not stroking his ego. The ultimate reality was that Haman's pride hung him on the gallows of his own making.

Behold, the wicked man conceives evil

and is pregnant with mischief

and gives birth to lies.

He makes a pit, digging it out,

and falls into the hole that he has made.

His mischief returns upon his own head,

and on his own skull his violence descends.

Psalm 7:14-16

In the last chapter, we discovered the connection between the original language from Esther 3:17 about the casting of the Pur and the phrasing from Esther 6:13 about Haman "surely coming to ruin," both defined as "dropping as in casting lots, casting down, falling prostrate to worship, and falling upon to attack."2 This is also the exact word used when Haman falls on the couch where Esther sat. Haman cast himself down. He fell upon her, either to worship or to attack—the motivation is unclear.

The Pur, or dice, that Haman first cast in Esther 3 was about his schemes for self-promotion and gain. But in the hands of the divine, these plans fell upon his own head, even as his ultimate fate was sealed when he fell upon the couch as the king was returning to the room.

Let us be encouraged about the very real enemy who comes against us. Lucifer was cast down from heaven due to his pride, and he will ultimately be banished from earth by the kingdom of God. The traps that he tries to set will fall upon himself, and he will be exposed as surely as Haman was. Though he uses the weapon of fear upon us, it is born of the terror he feels knowing that our King has already determined his end, depicted by how Haman was terrified before the king when his wickedness was uncovered (see Esther 7:6).

Haman plotted to hang his enemy on a pole to bring an end to the man he despised, exactly as our enemy thought the cross would bring him victory. In both instances, God had the last word and the wood of the enemy's making resulted in his own defeat.

Only Jesus

Mordecai advised his cousin, Esther, that she was divinely placed for "such a time as this" (Esther 4:14), with an invitation to partake in God's purposes. Esther chose to accept the summons to be part of God's redemption for the people of Israel, alluding to the Son of God who secured our redemption by following the will of his Father. Jesus is the fulfillment of every "if" statement that Esther utters to Ahasuerus as she offers her pleas. Because of Jesus, we need not ask if we have found favor or if the king is pleased, for Jesus answers any "if" that separates us from the grace of God and receiving his mercy.

Jesus Christ hung on a pole in our place, a painful and public death, in order to satisfy the debt of all sin. This moved us from the enemy of God, as Haman was to the Jews, to the bride of Christ, as Esther was the bride to Ahasuerus. The cross did not just free us from being slaves to sin, but it grants us eternal life because it is the plea that came before the Holy God and made a way for us to chase a better kingdom.

And if a man has committed a crime punishable by death and he is put to death, and you hang him on a tree, his body shall not remain all night on the tree, but you shall bury him the same day, for a hanged man is cursed by God.

Deuteronomy 23:22-23

For all the promises of God find their Yes in him. That is why it is through him that we utter our Amen to God for his glory. And it is God who establishes us with you in Christ, and has anointed us, and who has also put his seal on us and given us his Spirit in our hearts as a guarantee.

2 Corinthians 1:20-22

Response to Esther 7

The Word of God is meant to transform and call us to action. Take some time to consider the questions below and write out your responses.

• *Where do you feel captive in your life – to an idol or habit or hardship? What are the areas where you need God to move within you to find freedom?*

• *Is there an area in your life where you are struggling to hand it over to God's sovereignty or believe his goodness? What is it?*

• *What are the fears or worries that bring a sense of defeat? Has this chapter helped you to see this as a tactic of your enemy? Make it a habit to confess that worry to God in prayer every time it comes to mind – asking God to build your belief for him and confessing the unbelief that is the root of the worry.*

• *Is your life marked with a sense of freedom and victory because of the cross? This comes through our regular confession of our desperate need for it.*

The Truths of Esther 7

Let's wrap up this section of Scripture by considering these three elements.

1—Adoration of God from Esther 7

- You are the God who is approachable and available.

- You are the God who is personal and wants us to seek you.

- You are the God who is generous to free and save us through the cross.

- You are the God who is our deliverer from the plots of the enemy, redeeming us to become his bride.

- You are the God who is gracious and merciful beyond measure.

- You are the God who delights in relationship with us.

- You are the God who gives us belonging in your kingdom.

- You are the God who gave your Son to die on the pole of our sin's making.

- You are the God who is the defender of our cause.

- You are the God who is patient, just, and attentive.

2—Affirmation of Our Gospel Identity from Esther 7

- I once was an enemy but have been made a bride.

- I belong to the kingdom of God.

- I am a citizen of heaven and an alien in this world.

- I am a recipient of God's kindness and favor through Jesus.

- I am granted access to God through Jesus, the golden scepter.

- I am freed from the captivity of sin, including fear and worry.

- I am defended by God.

- I am shown grace because sin's curse and wrath were satisfied through the cross.

3—Actions to Take from Esther 7

- I am to prayer over my own life and plead for others in prayer.

- I am to be mindful of my true kingdom.

- I am to approach God humbly and with surrender in all requests, trusting his sovereignty and goodness, even when I cannot see it.

- I am to consider my own guilt in sinful actions and let God handle that of other people.

- I am to repent from arrogance and pride and self-glorification.

- I am to ever remember my undeserved position before God granted by grace.

Conclusion of Esther 7

This seventh chapter of Esther is not about a bad guy getting his due. It's a vivid representation of the totality of the gospel story. We are enemies made the bride of Christ. We are granted a position in the kingdom. We have received not only the golden scepter of access but also the cross that bought us out of the wages of our sin to life eternal. The enemy was defeated by the very wooden beam that he thought would bring him victory. No matter the plots coming against us on any given day, we can rest assured that our Heavenly Father hears our pleas, has secured our future, and has defended our cause. Whatever this life includes, Jesus declared that it is finished. Grace made a way for us to belong to an eternal kingdom.

GOSPEL STORY AS ILLUSTRATED IN ESTHER 7

ENEMY OF KING
like Haman

ME

--an enemy of God
--evil like Haman
--made a bride
--belong to a royal kingdom
--slave and condemned
--freed and saved
--redeemed and welcomed
--granted access through Jesus

JESUS

--fulfills the if for God's pleasure and favor
--the golden scepter allowing me to approach throne
--freed and SAVED me
--death on the cross covered the wrath from sins & moves me from enemy to bride

GOD THE FATHER

--enthroned above the universe
--wants relationship with us
--listens and invites us in
--delights to extend mercy & grace
--required Someone to hang a pole to fulfill wrath from sin
--defends our cause
--redeems us from evil

ENEMY

cast down by his own evil and defeated by the wood of his own scheming

ESTHER 8

"...for an edict written in the name of the king and sealed with the

king's ring cannot be revoked."

Esther 8:8b

Esther 8, *English Standard Version*

Esther Saves the Jews

8 On that day King Ahasuerus gave to Queen Esther the house of Haman, the enemy of the Jews. And Mordecai came before the king, for Esther had told what he was to her. 2 And the king took off his signet ring, which he had taken from Haman, and gave it to Mordecai. And Esther set Mordecai over the house of Haman.

3 Then Esther spoke again to the king. She fell at his feet and wept and pleaded with him to avert the evil plan of Haman the Agagite and the plot that he had devised against the Jews. 4 When the king held out the golden scepter to Esther, Esther rose and stood before the king. 5 And she said, "If it please the king, and if I have found favor in his sight, and if the thing seems right before the king, and I am pleasing in his eyes, let an order be written to revoke the letters devised by Haman the Agagite, the son of Hammedatha, which he wrote to destroy the Jews who are in all the provinces of the king. 6 For how can I bear to see the calamity that is coming to my people? Or how can I bear to see the destruction of my kindred?"7 Then King Ahasuerus said to Queen Esther and to

Mordecai the Jew, "Behold, I have given Esther the house of Haman, and they have hanged him on the gallows, because he intended to lay hands on the Jews. 8 But you may write as you please with regard to the Jews, in the name of the king, and seal it with the king's ring, for an edict written in the name of the king and sealed with the king's ring cannot be revoked."

9 The king's scribes were summoned at that time, in the third month, which is the month of Sivan, on the twenty-third day. And an edict was written, according to all that Mordecai commanded concerning the Jews, to the satraps and the governors and the officials of the provinces from India to Ethiopia, 127 provinces, to each province in its own script and to each people in its own language, and also to the Jews in their script and their language. 10 And he wrote in the name of King Ahasuerus and sealed it with the king's signet ring. Then he sent the letters by mounted couriers riding on swift horses that were used in the king's service, bred from the royal stud, 11 saying that the king allowed the Jews who were in every city to gather and defend their lives, to destroy, to kill, and to annihilate any armed force of any people or province that might attack them, children and women

included, and to plunder their goods, 12 on one day throughout all the provinces of King Ahasuerus, on the thirteenth day of the twelfth month, which is the month of Adar. 13 A copy of what was written was to be issued as a decree in every province, being publicly displayed to all peoples, and the Jews were to be ready on that day to take vengeance on their enemies. 14 So the couriers, mounted on their swift horses that were used in the king's service, rode out hurriedly, urged by the king's command. And the decree was issued in Susa the citadel.

15 Then Mordecai went out from the presence of the king in royal robes of blue and white, with a great golden crown and a robe of fine linen and purple, and the city of Susa shouted and rejoiced. 16 The Jews had light and gladness and joy and honor. 17 And in every province and in every city, wherever the king's command and his edict reached, there was gladness and joy among the Jews, a feast and a holiday. And many from the peoples of the country declared themselves Jews, for fear of the Jews had fallen on them.

THE WONDER OF THE NEW COVENANT
Esther 8

I've had the honor of being an adoption social worker for twenty-five years now. The majority of my career, I've worked as a contract home study caseworker for international adoptions. I'm the social worker who goes to the house for the initial report and then has the privilege of walking the family through their post-placement time, typically lasting one year after the adoption.

As I sat with a family a few years ago, we discussed their child's adjustment from an orphanage a world away to their comfortable suburban home. She was old enough to remember her life in the orphanage very vividly, living without a father or a mother to tuck her in. Yet, her "normal" was life in the orphanage, where the caring staff did all they could to nurture the little ones under their supervision.

Like many of the cases that I've worked on, the back story is one of poverty where an orphanage is essentially chosen by desperate

267

parents for the reassurance that at least their child is fed and safe. Within orphanages around the world, the children eventually age out, facing a bleak future of homelessness, substance abuse, victimization, and often early death.

This little girl's adoptive family intentionally jumped through all the hoops and endured the waiting to travel the globe and make her their own. The sudden loss of all that's familiar is terrifying and traumatic to kids. They're left with a sense of grief about the normal they knew, even though the new norm is one of plenty and security. Grasping their new identity is difficult at best.

This particular family began a daily ritual to help their daughter fully embrace who she had become through her adoption. When they tucked her in, holding her hand as she fell asleep, they would have her repeat out loud, "You are my mother, and you are my father. I am your daughter, and we are a forever family. This is who I am."

One would think that an orphan would eagerly step into their new name and new provision. But processing that dramatic change is nearly more than some of the children can handle, requiring help and often therapy.

How like us. We can sit in pews, read the Bible, attend Bible studies, and talk the Christian lingo, but do we truly and completely step into the identity we've been given by the new covenant? As you read through this chapter, hold fast to this truth.

When you choose to believe in and follow Jesus, this is your story. This is your Father. This is who he is, and his new covenant radically transforms your identity, purpose, and your eternal future. When we live in the fullness of this, others become hungry for what we have.

Our Adoptive Identity

As we learn to rehearse truths about God, we build our ability to believe our new identity so that we can step into it more fully. Like the little girl holding her new mother and father's hands, we intentionally tell ourselves *whose* we are, and this defines *who* we

are. We say it as often as we need to hear it, and, incrementally over

time, we are transformed to step into this identity with great

confidence. We can begin to live in a hearty belief our new story,

written through the blood of Jesus.

We become like that little girl who bloomed before my eyes over the

years that I worked with her family. Her transformation came only as

she learned to stitch together both her life before and her life now,

reconciling and honoring where she came from and embracing where

she lives now.

Who We Once Were

Many believers in Jesus live with one foot in old identities, old lies,

and old wounds and the other foot in a fleeting understanding of who

the triune God actually is—Father, Son, and Holy Spirit. This is the

best summation I can offer on how I feel I've missed the glory of

God for most of my life; I've spent so many decades trying to deny my depravity without Jesus that it was impossible to relish the wonder of him.

• Reflect on whether you tend to battle like an adoptee to fully rest in and embrace your identity in the kingdom of God or if you are often led by doubts, feelings, and circumstances of this life.

When I go to see a newly adopted child in the first month home, they tend to be either frenzied with nervous energy, fueled by fear and grief, or stoic and quiet with an almost glazed look in their eye. I could respond to this by telling them to relax because we've done our due diligence to check out this new mother and father. I could explain we've run background checks and gathered all sorts of documentation from financial statements to health reports to letters of reference. I could even let them read the lengthy home study report or read it to them in order to reassure them that this is a good and safe place to which they now belong.

However, no matter what I say or how much I smile, the children can only build confidence in their new parents by experience. They have to get to know them experientially. They have to learn, day by day, who these new people are in order to release preconceived ideas based on any traumatic past history.

Reconciling Our Sinful Past

The death of Haman became a turning point for Esther, finally freed from the enemy and enjoying full confidence in the king's presence. In fact, she and Mordecai found the courage to end the charade about their relationship, finally telling Ahasuerus "who Mordecai was to her," (Esther 8:1).

We, too, gain freedom and intimacy with our King, enjoying both full confidence in his presence and full freedom from the enemy, when we continually work to reconcile ourselves with our sinful nature. This ongoing awareness unlocks our ability to understand, believe, and appreciate the grace of God. We most fully embrace our assurance with God through Jesus when we most fully acknowledge our reality as sinners who only have access to the presence of God because of Jesus.

The spiritual habit of confession properly aligns our hearts to agree with God about our sinful ways, and it keeps us humbled at the ongoing forgiveness bought through the cross. Confession is the bridge that connects our past as doomed sinners to our new identity as forgiven and free. Confession also reminds us that our enemy, too, has been defeated. An astonishment for the cross is where we experience God in increasing measure, tying ourselves to the miracle of grace.

• *Do you tend to give yourself too much credit, or are you able to live in full awareness of your absolute dependence on God's grace?*

Though we live in want and may feel lonely, unclaimed, and abandoned with little to no chance to thrive, God the Father moved heaven and Earth to adopt us as sons and daughters. He is the God who says, "I am your Abba Father. You belong to my forever kingdom. Now stand firm in your faith and rest in the new covenant of grace."

Therefore, if anyone is in Christ, he is a new creation. The old has passed away; behold, the new has come.

2 Corinthians 5:17

To build a deep and abiding confidence in God, we must press forward with continual intention to know him more, mindful of our desperate need for him. Coupling knowledge of God on a surface level with unhurried experience with God is what establishes a transforming faith, where you can begin to rest in the freedom and vastness of his grace.

Therefore, since we have been justified by faith, we have peace with

God through our Lord Jesus Christ. Through him we have

also obtained access by faith into this grace in which we stand,

and we rejoice in hope of the glory of God.

Romans 5:1-2

Empowered by God's Authority

When King Ahasuerus gave his signet ring to Mordecai in Esther 8, he was offering the authority to act on the king's behalf. We, too, are equipped and empowered by God through the Holy Spirit given to his followers, as the Holy Spirit is the conduit of God's authority within us. He empowers and equips us daily in all we face and encounter. Surrendering ourselves to be led by the Holy Spirit within us is how we can continue to press forward to more abundant living as redeemed and rescued children of God.

Brothers, I do not consider that I have made it my own. But one

thing I do: forgetting what lies behind and straining forward to what lies ahead, I press on toward the goal for the prize of the

upward call of God in Christ Jesus.

Philippians 3:13 - 14

One privilege of this authority we've been given as children of God is pictured as Esther pleads for the lives of her people. We, likewise, are to plead and weep, bowing before the King, for the lives of others. To be intercessors is a high calling, yet we often forget and neglect this privilege by taking prayer for granted, using it as a last resort, rather than practicing it as a powerful spiritual discipline. Or, we selfishly use the practice of prayer for our own needs, neglecting to plead for the lives and rescue of others.

Let us work to have reverence for the ability to stand before the throne, firm in our faith, interceding not just for our own lives, but for the needs of others.

Let us rely on the Holy Spirit to help us understand God and his Word, and to direct and guide us, fueled by this power of God within us.

A Just Covenant Keeper

Esther was pleading with King Ahasuerus' fervently because of the law of the king could not be revoked. The same is true of God's law. Whereas Haman's death decree was issued for the Jews, mankind's death decree was issued when sin entered the world in the garden of Eden. In order to be just and righteous, God must uphold his law, requiring death for sin. Throughout the Old Testament, this obligation was fulfilled through the strict requirements of ongoing animal sacrifices, as well as obedience to the tedious Law given to the Israelites.

Ahasuerus' consent for a second decree foreshadows God's merciful solution for his ultimate counter-decree over sin and death. In the New Testament, our covenant keeper, Almighty God, shows both his absolute justice and his boundless mercy through the new decree offered through Jesus' death and resurrection, which overrode the death decree over us, and also fulfilled the law of God from the Old Testament. The lengths that the God of the Universe went to in order to secure our position as his forgiven children, with the penalty of our sins paid in full, should motivate us to live out that freedom wholly.

The adopted children I know who flourish the most are those who can connect with who they once were, while ever mindful of who their adoption has made them become, fully exercising their rights and privileges as children in their forever families. We, likewise, can thrive in our identity as adopted children of the Eternal Father.

Now before faith came, we were held captive under the law, imprisoned until the coming faith would be revealed. So then, the law was our guardian until Christ came, in order that we might be justified by faith. But now that faith has come, we are no longer under a guardian, for in Christ

Jesus you are all sons of God, through faith.

Galatians 3:23-26

A New Covenant, for All People

After the king's authorization, Mordecai had a copy of the newly issued decree sent to every province of the kingdom, commanding that it be publicly displayed and written in all languages for all people. As followers of Jesus, we, too, are called to share the incredibly good news of the adoption God offers, everywhere we go, all over the world.

"Go therefore and make disciples of all nations, baptizing them in the name of the Father and of the Son and of the Holy Spirit, teaching them to observe all that I have commanded you. And behold, I am with you always, to the end of the age."

Matthew 28:19 -20

The angels declared it from the minute that Jesus was born that the Son of God was good news for all people.

And the angel said to them, "Fear not, for behold,

I bring you good news of great joy that will be for

all the people. For unto you is born this day

in the city of David a Savior, who is Christ the Lord.

And this will be a sign for you:

you will find a baby wrapped in swaddling clothes

and lying in a manger."

Luke 2:10-12

The original death decree from Haman concerned the Jews in the kingdom, but the new decree was received joyfully even by non-Jews. This is a taste of the New Testament. Jesus came, not just to save the Jewish nation, but for all of us.

Living Joyfully as Overcomers

As the news of the new decree was swiftly announced throughout the kingdom of Ahasuerus, the Jews show us what it means to live as overcomers, counting on the promise of a new future. Two months after their death decree was issued, and still nine months minus ten days from the day of battle, they celebrated. They rejoiced with gladness and joy and light even though the dark day was still ahead. In fact, they rejoiced with a feast and a holiday, and it caused those around them to take notice to the point of claiming themselves to be Jews.

This is kingdom living in a broken messed up world with daily battles looming.

This is a life so centered on what the gospel decrees that we can find rest even as our battles loom before us, being assured that the ultimate and eternal victory is ours though it may be deferred.

No, in all these things
we are more than conquerors

It's not an overnight process to live out the promise as overcomers with eternal communion with God.

Just like the little adopted girl, we don't hop on a plane and leave all the smells, sounds, and sights that we've ever known as broken, sinful people and wake up the next day fully reconciled with our new identity as new creations, living it out with incredible joy. It's a slow and gradual process, day by day, to deliberately fix our thoughts on who the triune God is – Father, Son, and Holy Spirit. We invest time with him to know him better and love him more, intentionally seeking to build faith and confidence through our experience of him.

We are transformed by God as we seek him. We fix our eyes on him as often as we have to, setting before ourselves what we wish to become. Our work is to obey; his promise is to handle the results.

When we live as if Jesus is enough, others will take notice.

It's what our world is starving for, both inside the church and out.

Everyone longs for a fulfillment and satisfaction that is steadfast and unyielding, beyond emotions and circumstance. If our lives are to be marked with the side effect of grace and joy, we have to gain understanding, confidence, and acceptance of God's grace toward us beyond the facts of Christianity. We do this through intentional experience of the Lord. This is how we gradually live out the fullness of the remarkable, overriding new covenant.

Response to Esther 8

The Word of God is meant to transform and call us to action. Take some time to consider the questions below and write out your responses.

• *We are prone to question why bad things happen to good people. Yet, how often do you think about why God would dare to pardon your sins and free you from the death? Do you routinely feel in awe of his grace and mercy?*

• *What about God and the gospel story of his grace feels hard to believe?*

• *Where do you see yourself in the story of the adopted girl? On any given day, do you tend to relive the past or feel weighed down by it? Do you feel conflicted between the past and present? Do you feel dread or joy about the future?*

- *How fully would you say that you are able to experience God? How fully have you embraced your new identity in the new covenant, living with both an awareness of your state as a sinner and your eternal future because of your Savior?*

- *Is your life marked by a joy in your adoption by God the Father? Do others see something different in you because of your adoption to the kingdom of God – a life marked by joy, grace, and peace that is anchored in the enduring truths of an unchanging God?*

The Truths of Esther 8

Let's wrap up this section of Scripture by considering these three elements.

1—Adoration of God from Esther 8

- You are the God who adopted us as sons and daughters, willing to do what it required.

- You are the God of all authority, over all the earth.

- You are the God who is gracious and generous with mercy.

- You are the God who equips us with your authority and power through the Holy Spirit.

- You are the God who is just and holy.

- You are the God who requires that the penalty of sins be paid in full.

- You are the God who overruled the death decree for all through Jesus.

- You are the God who is the covenant keeper.

- You are the God who is powerful and personal.

- You are the God who is concerned for all.

- You are the God who is steadfast and faithful.

- You are the God who is our victory.

- You are the God who equips us to live with joy, knowing we have eternity.

- You are the God who is light in our darkness.

2—Affirmation of Our Gospel Identity from Esther 8

- I am saved, adopted, and given a new identity and new forever home.

- I am given God's authority and power through the Holy Spirit.

- I am equipped through the Holy Spirit.

- I am an intercessor.

- I am given honor as a co-heir with Christ in the kingdom of God.

- I am a new creation, freed from the death decree, an overcomer.

3—Actions to Take from Esther 8

- I am to plead and intercede for others, broken for them.

- I am to live under God's authority.

- I am to have urgency and eagerness to share the new covenant of the grace.

- I am to clothe myself every day in Christ, reminded of his righteousness that covers me.

- I am to rest in God's victory, even when it's deferred.

- I am to find joy in grace, embracing my new identity through Christ.

- I am to celebrate my life as a daughter of the King in such a way that there's an obvious difference to others.

Conclusion of Esther 8

Our sinful nature dooms us to death, but God, in his grace and mercy, maintained his justice and holiness while also offering the sacrifice required for our pardon. Our pride gets in the way of humbling ourselves to our justification through Jesus because it requires that we grieve and weep at the feet of our Holy God, that we admit our inability to earn his favor, and that we find the faith to reach out and touch the golden scepter. Yet a life reaching for the hem of Jesus is exactly how we can dare to stand before the King. A deep and transforming faith requires an ongoing humility. It requires a willingness to take the time to learn who God really is and to worship him by understanding his attributes and preaching them to ourselves. It requires a patience to actively seek to know him experientially. As stated previously, we cannot be revolutionized by our new identity through grace unless we are ever in awe of our desperate need for it. Knitting our thoughts and habits to our new identity in the "forever family of God" should cause transformation obvious to others, over time. It equips us to live differently as we fix our eyes on the unseen and greater kingdom. We can be less impacted by daily battles as we gain confidence in our ultimate victory. As we are freed, we are to bring freedom to others, eagerly helping them experience God through our actions and words.

ESTHER 9

...the reverse occurred...

Esther 9:1

Esther 9, *English Standard Version*

The Jews Destroy Their Enemies

9 Now in the twelfth month, which is the month of Adar, on the

thirteenth day of the same, when the king's command and edict were

about to be carried out, on the very day when the enemies of the

Jews hoped to gain the mastery over them, the reverse occurred: the

Jews gained mastery over those who hated them. 2 The Jews gathered

in their cities throughout all the provinces of King Ahasuerus to lay

hands on those who sought their harm. And no one could stand

against them, for the fear of them had fallen on all peoples. 3 All the

officials of the provinces and the satraps and the governors and the

royal agents also helped the Jews, for the fear of Mordecai had fallen

on them. 4 For Mordecai was great in the king's house, and his fame

spread throughout all the provinces, for the man Mordecai

grew more and more powerful. 5 The Jews struck all their enemies

with the sword, killing and destroying them, and did as they pleased

to those who hated them. 6 In Susa the citadel itself the Jews killed

and destroyed 500 men, 7 and also killed Parshandatha and Dalphon

and Aspatha 8 and Poratha and Adalia and Aridatha 9 and Parmashta and Arisai and Aridai and Vaizatha, 10 the ten sons of Haman the son of Hammedatha, the enemy of the Jews, but they laid no hand on the plunder.

11 That very day the number of those killed in Susa the citadel was reported to the king. 12 And the king said to Queen Esther, "In Susa the citadel the Jews have killed and destroyed 500 men and also the ten sons of Haman. What then have they done in the rest of the king's provinces! Now what is your wish? It shall be granted you. And what further is your request? It shall be fulfilled." 13 And Esther said, "If it please the king, let the Jews who are in Susa be allowed tomorrow also to do according to this day's edict. And let the ten sons of Haman be hanged on the gallows." 14 So the king commanded this to be done. A decree was issued in Susa, and the ten sons of Haman were hanged. 15 The Jews who were in Susa gathered also on the fourteenth day of the month of Adar and they killed 300 men in Susa, but they laid no hands on the plunder.

16 Now the rest of the Jews who were in the king's provinces also gathered to defend their lives, and got relief from their enemies

and killed 75,000 of those who hated them, but they laid no hands on the plunder. 17 This was on the thirteenth day of the month of Adar, and on the fourteenth day they rested and made that a day of feasting and gladness. 18 But the Jews who were in Susa gathered on the thirteenth day and on the fourteenth, and rested on the fifteenth day, making that a day of feasting and gladness. 19 Therefore the Jews of the villages, who live in the rural towns, hold the fourteenth day of the month of Adar as a day for gladness and feasting, as a holiday, and as a day on which they send gifts of food to one another.

The Feast of Purim Inaugurated

20 And Mordecai recorded these things and sent letters to all the Jews who were in all the provinces of King Ahasuerus, both near and far, 21 obliging them to keep the fourteenth day of the month Adar and also the fifteenth day of the same, year by year, 22 as the days on which the Jews got relief from their enemies, and as the month that had been turned for them from sorrow into gladness and from mourning into a holiday; that they should make them days of feasting

and gladness, days for sending gifts of food to one another and gifts to the poor.

23 So the Jews accepted what they had started to do, and what Mordecai had written to them. 24 For Haman the Agagite, the son of Hammedatha, the enemy of all the Jews, had plotted against the Jews to destroy them, and had cast Pur (that is, cast lots), to crush and to destroy them. 25 But when it came before the king, he gave orders in writing that his evil plan that he had devised against the Jews should return on his own head, and that he and his sons should be hanged on the gallows. 26 Therefore they called these days Purim, after the term Pur. Therefore, because of all that was written in this letter, and of what they had faced in this matter, and of what had happened to them, 27 the Jews firmly obligated themselves and their offspring and all who joined them, that without fail they would keep these two days according to what was written and at the time appointed every year, 28 that these days should be remembered and kept throughout every generation, in every clan, province, and city, and that these days of Purim should never fall into disuse among the Jews, nor

should the commemoration of these days cease among their descendants.

29 Then Queen Esther, the daughter of Abihail, and Mordecai the Jew gave full written authority, confirming this second letter about Purim. 30 Letters were sent to all the Jews, to the 127 provinces of the kingdom of Ahasuerus, in words of peace and truth, 31 that these days of Purim should be observed at their appointed seasons, as Mordecai the Jew and Queen Esther obligated them, and as they had obligated themselves and their offspring, with regard to their fasts and their lamenting. 32 The command of Esther confirmed these practices of Purim, and it was recorded in writing.

THE TRUEST REALITY

Esther 9

The thing about depression is that it when it takes root, it spreads through your thoughts and feelings like weeds. It chokes out the sun and steals all the water, growing bigger and lying to you about your life. For me, it bossed me around saying I was uninvited and rejected. It shaded everything until all the color ran out and life felt like an endless, staticky black and white rerun with nothing but hues of gray. This became the filter through which I saw my past, my every day, and the endless consuming future with no hint of vibrancy.

What you perceive becomes your reality, and the problem is that we so often color our world with misperceptions. In June 2018, I finally told my doctor that I felt as though I were constantly chasing away a black cloud that wanted to consume me. It included the heaviness of past wounds and a dread for the future. Only after he began treating my depression could I begin to catch glimpses of the truth. Only when I began to feel like myself again could I see how very unlike myself I had been. Gradually, the footing of the true reality began to take hold and the weighty burden lifted.

So often that's how we learn the most profound lessons. We experience dark places and feel alone, seeing no light at the end of an endless tunnel. It likes to deceive us that this is all that there will ever be. Dark, hard, heavy, overwhelming.

But it's not true. As Moses begged to see the glory of God in Exodus 33, we want to feel something that will break through it. We feel a need to witness with our own eyes what hope is and to hear an audible voice from heaven. Yet God responded to Moses' request by placing him in the dark cleft of a rock, covered by his hand, as his glory passed by: "Then, I will remove my hand you will see my back; but my face must not be seen" (Exodus 33:23).

What feels dark and lonely and hopeless might actually be the truest reality passing by, which we can only see in the aftermath. That's how revelations of God's glory often work. For me, this year has included these tiny pieces of evidence of God at work, such as being asked to lead a small group discussion for a women's Bible study. This might not seem like a big deal, but for me, a year prior, I wouldn't have fathomed that I had the bandwidth to step out, lead, and connect in such a social setting—or to write this book that you hold in your hands.

It took the hard season of being pruned in relationships, positions, ministries, and misperceptions to grasp the wonder of God's Word and the gospel story of grace and grace alone. I could not have imagined that God would grant me the privilege of stewarding the lessons he's taught me to share with others.

The truest reality is this. God is the Master and Author of our faith. Following Jesus means we will be taught, disciplined, and held. We just don't always feel the holding until the discipline, or the trial is over. Then, we look back and see how it was all being woven together. We battle and fight and feel defeated and press on, and our God wastes not one tear for his glory.

When I was a nineteen-year-old college sophomore, suddenly without parental support and experiencing deep grief, I put one foot in front of the other, stumbling to hold it together. Today, my forty-eight-year-old self wants to cheer that girl on and whisper to her that someday, when she becomes a college mom, God will connect all these dots and do something with it. He will take the idea of creating care packages with other college moms and grow it to be something he's dreamed. The joy that I feel since starting my Box Club organization in 2017 is the wonder from pains twenty-seven years ago that are now being knit together into redemption, building a college mom community offering college student support.

In whatever battle you are fighting, consider the truest reality we learn from Esther 9 and 10 and let it offer footholds as you keep climbing up the wall of the pit.

Our God is a Table Turner

Exiled from their homeland due to their idol worship and
disobedience to God's command, the destruction of the entire nation
of Israel had been set by the evil Haman and sealed with the king's
signet ring. The thirteenth day of the twelfth month of Adar was the
day of death.

But God.

Now in the twelfth month, which is the month of Adar, on the

thirteenth day of the same, when the king's command and edict

were about to be carried out, on the very day when the enemies of

the Jews hoped to gain the mastery over them, the reverse

occurred: the Jews gained mastery over those who hated them.

Esther 9:1

• *What certain death or circumstance has taken you captive? What is*

trying to gain—or is succeeding in gaining—mastery over you? What fears, worries, trials, and circumstances are filling your thoughts,

feeding your feelings, and consuming your life?

These things with which we struggle like to take hold and boss us around, and our natural response is to listen. We listen to the voice that paints a downward spiral outcome from what is happening right now. We imagine the worst. We hear the voice of the enemy when someone speaks negatively, harshly, or downright hatefully toward us. When the bills pile up, we imagine financial ruin. When the diagnosis is grim, we are overcome. When the relationship turns south, we see no chance of hope.

But our God is a table turner. Our God takes the ashes and creates beauty. Our God takes the sorrow and threats and calls us to depend on him. When circumstances bring us to the end of ourselves, we will find the Lord God Almighty as the knot in our rope.

I don't agree that God won't give you more than you can handle. He does, and he will. But you will never, not once, find yourself facing more than he can handle. Whatever hopes to gain mastery over you, it cannot stand because it cannot gain mastery over the sovereign God. He is the one who turns the tables, and, through him, we are readied for battle.

And no one could stand against them,

for the fear of them

had fallen on all peoples.

Esther 9:2

And my tongue will talk of your righteous help

all the day long, for they have been put

to shame and disappointed

who sought to do me hurt.

Psalm 71:24

Esther, Mordecai, and all the Jewish people in the kingdom of King Ahasuerus were real people facing real enemies. They had been exiled from their country because of their own defiance to God's laws. And yet, ultimately, no one could stand against them. Though God in his justice had allowed consequences for their rebellious idol worship and defiance when warned, he also responded with mercy, grace, and love to their petitions of dependence.

To give you truths to preach to yourself, consider these examples of how God turns the tables and causes the reverse to happen when harm is threatened.

Goliath taunted the Israeli army, causing them to shake in their boots. But God turned the tables, and a little shepherd boy used some rocks and a slingshot through the power of God to defeat the Philistines (1 Samuel 17).

For 400 years, the Jewish people were slaves in Egypt. Pharaoh was so scared that he demanded all Jewish boys be killed. Yet two Hebrew midwives refused to obey, and so a little boy named Moses survived. None of those enslaved Jews could have imagined that God would turn the tables, and they would leave captivity in Egypt with the plunder handed to them by the Egyptians before they escaped on dry land through the middle of the Red Sea (Exodus 1-15).

Gideon had three hundred men, with empty jars, trumpets, and torches, to fight against the vast Midianite army. God turned the table and reversed the circumstance so that numbers and weapons didn't matter, and the Midianites ran, crying out as they fled (Judges 7:21).

God took the barren Sarah and birthed descendants too numerous to count. He took the littlest son and made him the great King David.

He took the defiant Jonah and brought the Ninevites to repentance.

He used the widowed Moabite to become the grandmother of David.

He used a prostitute to save the spies and eventually bring the

destruction of Jericho.

Whatever is gaining mastery over you and causing you to listen to it

in despair, speak these verses over it prayerfully. Quit listening and

start talking to yourself with these examples of God's omnipotence.

Surely, Mordecai spoke the promises of God to himself, and it

equipped him to advise Esther to approach the king unsummoned

because "relief and deliverance will rise for the Jews" (Esther 4:14).

What then shall we say to these things?

If God is for us, who can be against us?

Romans 8:31

"I have said these things to you, that in me you may have peace. In the world you will have tribulation. But take heart; I have overcome the world."

John 16:33

No, in all these things we are more than conquerors through him who loved us. For I am sure that neither death nor life, nor angels nor rulers, nor things present nor things to come, nor powers, nor height nor depth, nor anything else in all creation, will be able to separate us from the love of God in Christ Jesus our Lord.

Romans 8:37-39

Battle in Community

The Jews fought back. But before there was ever a battle plan, they carefully took an important first step as a community of believers in God.

Then Esther told them to reply to Mordecai, "Go, gather all the Jews to be found in Susa, and hold a fast on my behalf, and do not eat or drink for three days, night or day. I and my young women will also fast as you do. Then I will go to the king, though it is against the law, and if I perish, I perish." Mordecai then went away and did everything as Esther had ordered him.

Esther 4:15-17

They wept in sackcloth and ashes, brought low with shock and fear. Then, they moved to their knees before acting, fasting and praying - turning their eyes to their Almighty God. They wept together and prayed together, and then they fought together.

Community is a necessary component to effectively face any battle. Esther 9:2 says the Jews assembled. In verse 15, the Jews in Susa came together, and then, in verse 18, they assembled on the thirteenth and the fourteenth day of Adar to fight and again on the fifteenth day to rest.

When it comes to living in community, I believe the people of the Church at large can do a far better job at reaching into the lives of the hurting both within our particular flocks and within our community. In our busy lives, we tell people to let us know if they need anything. We mean it sincerely. I know because I've said it.

But I also know that when I am wounded and paralyzed from battles in life, I can hardly summon the strength to cry out for help. No one on the battlefield of an actual war is expected to stand up and get themselves to the medics when they are bleeding out. The medics come to them. Triage comes to right where they've fallen down to assess and treat and then to transfer them to better care.

Community reaches out and shows up and assembles together to mount an attack so that we are able to help each other fight, equipped by the power of the God who leads us. We do so by creating a meal train during death and sickness. We send text messages and snail mail notes of encouragement. We sit in chemo treatment rooms, holding hands and passing the time. Though technology can be detrimental to actual and genuine community, it can also be a useful tool for helping others. We can send meal delivery gift cards through email or send grocery deliveries through internet shopping. We stay close enough to assess the needs and figure out how to meet them. When it's more than we can bear, we rally cry for others to join in, and we help connect our community to other resources.

Outside of our church circles, we reach those we don't know by chatting up the cashier and engaging with the people we encounter. Within our circles, we do the hard work to be vulnerable with our own needs and to keep at it when it gets hard. We are also to have realistic expectations of our community when we are in need, for only God himself will never disappoint us. Our community is neither our savior nor our fix. When we are in painful situations, let us not expect broken people to fill all our needs or assign to them what only God can do.

Relationships aren't easy to maintain, and we can tend to be consumers of each other and of our churches, seeking only to have our needs met rather than being people who live out the grace shown us. We must love the Bridegroom enough to stay faithful in loving his people, resting in God's mercy so wholeheartedly that we can extend it to each other.

One of the most beautiful examples of fighting in community is found in Exodus 17:8-16. The Israelites were battling the Amalekites in this passage, and, as long as Moses held up his arms, the Jews were winning. When he tired and his arms sagged, the Amalekites were prevailing. The battle was ultimately won because Aaron and Hur stood on each side of Moses to hold up his arms until sundown. This is a picture of holding each other up both literally and figuratively through prayer. It may feel like an inconvenience, but God calls us to it as a privilege of belonging to him.

Commemorate Every Win

In Esther 8, the Jews celebrated even before the victory, when the battle was still on its way. In Esther 9, they celebrated after the victory. God's commands within Leviticus and Deuteronomy are full of instructions about regular rhythms of celebration, feasting, and rest as the cornerstone of commemorating how God has shown up.

These practices call us to pause with praise and to worship our Father because he delights in and inhabits the praises of his people. It also encourages us to build our faith as we set milestones for God's faithfulness. Stopping life to feast with joy in community for his deliverance and victory is the single most powerful way to guard against spiritual forgetfulness.

We are all prone to it. In Matthew 14, the disciples witnessed Jesus break the bread and fish and feed the crowd of five thousand. Immediately after that, he walked on the water toward their boat, and he calmed the sea and storm. They worshiped him and proclaimed, "Truly you are the Son of God! (Matthew 14:33)." Then, within days, the disciples find themselves on another hillside with a hungry crowd.

Then Jesus called his disciples to him and said, "I have compassion on the crowd because they have been with me now three days and have nothing to eat. And I am unwilling to send them away hungry, lest they faint on the way." And the disciples said to him, "Where are we to get enough bread in such a desolate place to feed so great a crowd?"

Matthew 15:32-33

Womp, womp. I love the disciples because I see myself in them. They have, with their own eyes, seen Jesus feed thousands of people. They've worshiped and declared he is the Son of God. They've watched miraculous healings and seen nature obey Jesus' command. Just days later, they are literally locking eyes with the Bread of Life and asking where on earth they will get bread for the crowd. As I recognize my own habit of spiritual amnesia within the disciples, I am so encouraged by the response of our Savior.

He keeps showing up anyway. He repeats the miracle and feeds another crowd.

This is the underlying importance in events such as the festival of Purim. We carve out intentional ways to gather together and sing our songs of rescue to fill our souls and starve our doubts. These customs and rituals were established and commanded to be observed without fail because God knows how quickly we forget.

The One who knit us together asks that we build our belief in him for ourselves, for others, and for future generations by telling our God stories. We write them down to help us remember, in journals or on slips of paper, so that we can go back with evidence of what to tell our souls when we are prone to just listen to our struggling self. Noting the tiny wins along the way is a compelling way to heal the unbelief that feeds our worry.

Nothing Can Ultimately Defeat Us

I'm writing this chapter during the season of Lent, evidence of divine timing, as I gain a fresh perspective on Jesus' crucifixion and resurrection through the ninth chapter of Esther.

But when it came before the king, he gave orders in writing that his evil plan that he had devised against the Jews should return on his own head, and that he and his sons should be hanged on the gallows.

Esther 9:25

The enemy plotted against God's people. When this came to the king's attention, he issued a new command that this scheme would come back on his own head in ultimate defeat.

The LORD God said to the serpent, "Because you have done this, cursed are you above all livestock and above all beasts of the field;

on your belly you shall go,

and dust you shall eat

all the days of your life.

I will put enmity between you and the woman,

and between your offspring and her offspring;

he shall bruise your head,

and you shall bruise his heel."

Genesis 3:14-15

An attack was mounted, and the result was a death decree. Yet, in hindsight, through God's glorious and sovereign plan, this attack was actually ushering in the fulfillment of God's promises through a new, overriding covenant.

Belonging to God brings attack and enemies. This has always been true, not just for God's people, but even for God's Son. God promised through covenants with Abraham, Noah, and Moses that he would save his people and restore them. This plan of Haman's came back on his own head because God had a bigger plan to show his faithfulness.

Our current day battles are no different. We may feel the attack of man or attacks on our health, family, and relationships. Circumstances come against us, and it is not unlike the initial death decree issued in Susa. Except for one thing.

What God said in Genesis to the serpent was a promise that he kept. Though we feel tricked, deceived, and defeated, the promises of God through the life, death, and resurrection of Jesus tell the truest reality. Though the enemy struck Jesus on the heel and he was hanged on a pole, under the full weight of the curse of God as he carried our sin, the enemy was crushed. We can find hope in the hardest of times when we anchor it all to the nothingness of an empty tomb.

As followers of Jesus, nothing can separate us from the love of God "because death couldn't hold him, and the grave couldn't have him."[1] Jesus had the last word when he announced it is finished and he promised he would come back.

He is, you know. Jesus is coming back to earth. We belong to an unshakeable kingdom, and death does not get the last word. Though our earthly lives will end, we have been made co-heirs with Christ, and there is a never-ending kingdom where we will reign beside him. This is where I found hope to say whether my dad lived or died from his cancer, he would be healed completely. This is where we lay a foundation of faith that can declare, in all seasons, "The joy of the Lord is my strength" (Nehemiah 8:10). This is living out with confidence that Jesus is enough.

Though we weep and mourn and lie in sackcloth, when we are clothed in garments of salvation, we can rest assured that no matter what comes against us in this world, it doesn't have the last word.

The celebration of Purim, commemorating the remarkable victory of the exiled Jews within the kingdom of Ahasuerus, is to include times of fasting and lamentation as well as feasting and joy. The sacrament of communion is a picture of this. It is a meal of remembrance with a cup and the bread, remembering the blood spilled and the body broken for our eternal gain.

This is the gospel story. We are doomed to die because of our sin. But a new covenant was written, and the victory of the empty tomb came only after the bitter tears of a horrible death. Though we do not see it, we can throw all our hopes into that nothingness of the empty tomb, daring ourselves to look beyond the here and now to a promised forever with the King of Kings.

Response to Esther 9

The Word of God is meant to transform and call us to action. Take some time to consider the questions below and write out your responses.

• *Was there anything in this chapter that spoke to you about a battle you're facing? Do you generally see yourself as equipped by the*

Almighty God for each day or as weighed down by the circumstances of each day?

• *Consider your weekly routine. Do you have intentional times of interacting with others to encourage and help each other, rallying together? If not, who can you prayerfully consider building such relationships with and how?*

• *In light of the biggest battle you are facing, stop to remember how God has shown up in your life in similar struggles in the past. Write these down to read regularly.*

• *Can you believe that the same God who reversed the fate of the Jews is using your own battles for ultimate victory? Can you find hope in an empty tomb that gives us hope against even the threat of death?*

• *Sometimes God allows us to see how he connects the dots to redeem our struggles for good. Stop and think about how this has been true in your own life and think of the fact that in heaven we will fully understand how God was always at work in our lives for his glory and our holiness.*

The Truths of Esther 9

Let's wrap up this section of Scripture by considering these three elements.

1—Adoration of God from Esther 9

- You are the God who is the table turner and who reverses our circumstances.

- You are the God who is our ultimate victory.

- You are the God who is our hope and way maker.

- You are the God who is our defender and protector.

- You are the God who goes before us in battle and equips us for our battles.

- You are the God who is our refuge, relief, and deliverance.

- You are the God who is our rest at a soul level.

- You are the God who redeems our experiences.

- You are the God who brings joy and feasting.

- You are the God who is praiseworthy and trustworthy.

- You are the God who is our peace, truth, and assurance.

- You are the God who is our freedom.

- You are the God who is good and faithful.

- You are the God who defeated death and sin.

- You are the ONE who is enough.

2—Affirmation of Our Gospel Identity from Esther 9

- I am an overcomer, victorious through Jesus with life eternal.

- I am equipped and called, readied for battle.

- I am seen and heard.

- I am a warrior, equipped with the armor of God (Ephesians 6).

- I am rich in the kingdom, with no need for earthly plunder.

- I am a child of God, loved and adopted.

- I belong to an unshakable kingdom.

- I am promised an everlasting future.

- I have access to God.

3—Actions to Take from Esther 9

- I am to wait on the Lord.

- I am to trust his power and love.

- I am to obey him and trust his provision.

- I am to be bold and brave.

- I am to know, rest, and remember his promises.

- I am to celebrate and tell of his faithfulness.

- I am to be intentional to battle against spiritual amnesia.

Conclusion of Esther 9

Ours is a story of certain defeat, weeping in sackcloth and ashes, were it not for the intervention of a powerful king with a new covenant plan to reverse the schemes of the enemy. From the beginning of time, our enemy has been working within the constraints of our sovereign God on borrowed time. Though his lies and strategies have never changed, we continue to be tripped up by them.

Such is life in a fallen world. We must intentionally bring to mind the ultimate reality, though it is foggy and unclear. Faith is a choice to trust, and belief is built stone by stone, requiring reconstruction when circumstances knock it down. The beauty of every word of the Bible is that it is all connected, God-inspired, and tells us repeatedly what God did for us because of who he is. It has nothing to do with our capabilities or track records. Grace is an endless ocean with limitless and unsearchable depths.

THE CONCLUSION: ESTHER 10

And Mordecai sent letters to all the Jews in the 127 provinces of

Ahasuerus' kingdom – words of goodwill and assurance.

Esther 9:30, NIV

Esther 10, *English Standard Version*

The Greatness of Mordecai

10 King Ahasuerus imposed tax on the land and on the coastlands of the sea. 2 And all the acts of his power and might, and the full account of the high honor of Mordecai, to which the king advanced him, are they not written in the Book of the Chronicles of the kings of Media and Persia? 3 For Mordecai the Jew was second in rank to King Ahasuerus, and he was great among the Jews and popular with the multitude of his brothers, for he sought the welfare of his people and spoke peace to all his people.

THE SUM OF OUR LIVES

Esther 10

A few years back, my sister and her family lost a friend in a car accident. While I can't recall meeting him, I can't forget what my sister told me about his life philosophy— "finish empty." Though he died too soon, he lived with a clear purpose. Through the faith transformation of the last few years in my own life, continually working to grow in understanding grace and release the burdens of legalism, I have found great incentive in this two-word phrase.

Finish empty.

We will all finish. One way or another, we will run, stumble, crawl, and finish the race of this life. In increasing measure, I find myself wanting to use my days, time, and talents with eternal purpose. More and more, I see the emptiness of status and wealth in light of heaven. I am growing in sensitivity to when I try to steal God's glory for my own and am gaining perspective on aligning my motivations and thoughts with God's promises and commands.

It's so incrementally gradual that the sum effect is nearly imperceptible. We live in an instant world with grand results, but that's not the way of the kingdom. Instead, God calls us to live like Mordecai, sitting at the gate, day after day, and clinging to the faith of our fathers in a foreign land with a determination that will choose faith over fear, no matter the threat.

Like Mordecai, we go about our daily rhythms, connected to our relationship with God and choosing the kingdom thing, whether anyone notices or not. We speak up when we see threats against someone. We pace back and forth with great care and concern for our relatives and others. Over and again, we refuse to bow to culture, even when we know it could cost us everything.

When certain disaster looms, we weep and mourn and recall the promises of God that have never failed. These truths equip us to boldly take our place in his deliverance for others, even though we may perish.

When great honor and recognition come our way, we also do as Mordecai. We just return to our gatekeeping, day by day, joining with others, to follow and trust the God of the nations with a humility that understands that we seek to finish empty — throwing it all to the kingdom to come. Because when I see his face, I want to tell him I have nothing left to give rather than realizing what I held back.

What Letter Does Our Life Send?

At the end of Esther 9, Mordecai, then second in command in the entire kingdom of Ahasuerus, sent letters to all the Jews with words of peace and truth, or "goodwill and assurance," (vs. 30, NIV). At that point, in a position of great honor and power, Mordecai looked to the greater good. He looked beyond himself with a heart attuned to the needs of the people around him.

Though he sent actual letters, I wonder what figurative letters our lives send to those around us through our texts, conversations, social media posts, and interactions. Do we speak goodwill, peace, truth, grace, and assurances? Does our life give evidence to which kingdom we belong?

I wonder if I face my daily battles and my big struggles in such a way that others see a hope built on something yet to come.

I look to Mordecai, who chose to act in absolute confidence that since God said he would deliver his people, he could dare to ask his beloved Esther to risk death.

I look to Esther, who wrestled with fear and then chose to pray and believe that if she perished, she would perish, but she would obey no matter what.

I consider the Jews, who were ripped from the safety of their Jerusalem and the presence of God in their temple and moved to a foreign land. How easy it would be to melt into the opposing culture, which some Jews did. Yet there were those who said they would cling to the faith of their fathers and to the traditions and words of the Yahweh God, recalling the ways God had moved previously in order to find the courage to press on.

The fact that the Jews responded to the second decree, overriding Haman's death sentence, with feasting and celebration, though the battle lay ahead, is something to contemplate. My death decree has been overridden, through the blood of Christ, yet rather than looking to the ultimate victory to find joy, I tend to get stuck on the battles in between.

But we don't live under that Law. We've been given a new covenant that invites us to feast on grace, dining with the King as he transforms me. We are being changed and have a reserved seat at the Wedding Banquet of the Lamb when we are glorified to reign with Christ.

The book of Esther illustrates the gospel story over and again.

What the law demands is our banishment from the king's presence and for us to be stripped of all privilege because of our defiance. We have earned the payment that the law required as seen in the death decree. But the Son of God himself hung on the wooden pole, defined as a curse of God, took on the curse of sin, and abated the wrath of God for all the sin of all mankind.

This broke the death decree over us once and for all, and a new covenant was issued that brings ultimate hope and victory. The scheme of the enemy to use the wood for his own gain became his very defeat. God invites us to the approach the throne confidently through the golden scepter of Jesus.

Through this new covenant, we can find joy, even as battles loom. Because he is the God of deliverance who equips his people for battle and, even more unbelievable, he battles for us.

Though death may have its sting, it has been swallowed up in victory secured through Jesus, and we become children of God. We are clothed in garments of salvation, and someday we will be crowned eternally and will rule and reign with Jesus, as Mordecai took his place next to Ahasuerus.

We are invited, transformed, forgiven, radically changed, welcomed, saved, delighted in, given the honor of righteousness, and offered all hope, all joy, and all peace. All enemies have been defeated—sin, death, and man's opposition, lowly status, waning approval, and the need to strive.

Esther 10 summarizes a life of greatness—a life recorded in the Book of the Chronicles. Mordecai was considered great among the Jews and the multitudes because of how he finished empty. He spent his days, from gatekeeper to a position of second in command, "seeking the welfare of his people and speaking peace to all his people" (vs. 3). Mordecai lived out the call of this Scripture:

Therefore, my beloved brothers, be steadfast, immovable, always abounding in the work of the Lord, knowing that in the Lord your labor is not in vain.

1 Corinthians 15:58

Living for the Lord means being steadfast, immovable, always abounding the work of the Lord, knowing that all effort and all labor is not in vain. We are crowned and robed by the King, and he gives us a position in his eternal plans, daring to partner with us. Even the sermon I heard this very morning offers great instruction for applying these lessons we learn from Mordecai and Esther:

> We can live as joyfully pessimistic. [Living out our hardest life now, because we know the best life is to come]. We can find magnificence in the mundane. We can live with resiliency as we disentangle ourselves from rewards or fruit now, because we know a reward is coming. We can be fiercely realistic and be assured that God rewards faithfulness and not fruitfulness. We can be, as Charles Spurgeon notes, "like cedars rocked in a storm, but not uprooted." [1]

The unfathomable story of the gospel informs our identity as those rescued from death, and this defines our purpose. A great life that finishes empty is one that seeks the welfare of people and speaks God's peace to all people.

This is how we chase the kingdom.

My prayer for you, as we close our time together and as you continue your own faith journey, comes from Colossians 1:

We [I] continually ask God to fill you

with the knowledge of his will

through all the wisdom and understanding

that the Spirit gives,

so that you may live a life worthy of the Lord

and please him in every way:

bearing fruit in every good work,

growing in the knowledge of God,

being strengthened with all power

according to his glorious might

so that you may have great endurance and patience,

and giving joyful thanks to the Father,

who has qualified you to share

in the inheritance of his holy people in the kingdom of light.

Verses 9b - 12

Thank you for joining me on this walk through the book of Esther. I'm praying you are forever changed, knowing He is the God who fully equips you and who delights in YOU.

ACKNOWLEDGMENTS

God wastes nothing, and there are no words or acts of worship and surrender that are worthy enough for a Father who knows every detail about me and loves me still. He is the God who has held me every day of my life, even when it felt like this couldn't be true. Often only in hindsight can we see the glory of the ways he was weaving our mess into something else. I am awed that he would so patiently lead and love until I finally grasped the miracle of grace, which was a miracle I had missed in a lifetime of being a Christian. But now I know. Through a desert and wilderness, he was lovingly removing distractions, relationships, and positions so I could see him more clearly. This Great Awakening to grace has required me to posture my heart to bow low before I could see his majesty and splendor. May I steward well the lessons he's taught me, through this book and any other way that he invites me to partner with him for the cause of the kingdom.

Chris: You are the best man I know. You have demonstrated the unconditional love of God through your love for me all these years. I still cannot believe that you fell in love with me when I was at my worst, and that you continue to do so. You are my best friend, my gracious support system, and the love of my life. Forever and ever amen.

Collin, Cooper, and Caris: It's a miraculous thing to be your biggest fan, and then have you all cheer your mama on as I've chased this book, chased my dreams, and pursued our Lord. Thank you for enduring my season of depression and anxiety. Thank you for the hours you've allowed me to sit and type and read and study, even at the cost of homemade meals or time together. Being your mom is the highest honor and calling. I love seeing the people you are becoming – you are my favorite people! I love you each to the moon and back. I love and adore you!

Prologue to the Book of Esther

1. Dictionary.com, "Ahasuerus," accessed August 26, 2019, https://www.dictionary.com/browse/ahasuerus?s=t.

2. Naamah Green, "13 Things You Didn't Know About Queen Esther," Hidabroot: World's Largest Jewish TV Network, https://www.hidabroot.com/article/192836/13-Things-You-Didnt-Know-About-Queen-Esther.

Introduction to the Book of Esther

1. JR Vassar, sermons and teachings (paraphrased) at Church at the Cross, Grapevine.

2. JR Vassar, *Glory Hunger,* (Crossway Books, 2015).

Esther 1: If Not for God

1. Wildolive.co.uk, "Jewish Weddings," accessed February 2, 2019, http://www.wildolive.co.uk/weddings.htm.

2.. Hebrew-Greek Key Word Study Bible, NIV New International Version, 1984 Edition, "as he wished," AMG International Inc, 1996, p. 2015.

Esther 2: The Now and the Yet to Come

1. John Wesley, "Explanatory Notes on the Whole Bible," Sacred Text, http://mail.sacred-texts.com/bib/cmt/wesley/est002.htm.

2. Merriam-Webster Online, "beautify," accessed March 4, 2019, https://www.merriam-webster.com/dictionary/beautify.

Esther 3: A Faithful Life

1. Matthew Henry, "Bible Commentary (complete): Esther 3," Biblestudytools.com, https://www.biblestudytools.com/commentaries/matthew-henry-complete/esther/3.html.

2. DoSomething.org, "11 Facts About Global Poverty," accessed March 27, 2019, https://www.dosomething.org/us/facts/11-facts-about-global-poverty.

Esther 4: The Day of Devastation

1. JewBelong.com, "Death and Mourning: Shiva," accessed August 24, 2019, https://www.jewbelong.com/lifecycle/death/?gclid=EAIaIQobCh MIv6yn_oic5AIVmojICh3vMgj3EAAYASAAEgK0r_D_BwE#se ction4.

2. Hebrew-Greek Key Word Study Bible, NIV New International Version, 1984 Edition, "put to death," AMG International Inc, 1996, p. 1963.

3. Dictionary.com, "intercede," accessed March 21, 2019, https://www.dictionary.com/browse/intercede.

4. Hebrew-Greek Key Word Study Bible, NIV New International Version, 1984 Edition, "her people," AMG International Inc, 1996, p. 1991.

5. JR Vassar, "By the Grace of God", *Raised Sermon Series*, Church at the Cross, May 12, 2019, available on Church at the Cross website, https://churchatthecross.com/raised.

Esther 5: Battle Ready

1. Naamah Green, "13 Things You Didn't Know About Queen Esther," Hidabroot: World's Largest Jewish TV Network, https://www.hidabroot.com/article/192836/13-Things-You-Didnt-Know-About-Queen-Esther.

2. Naamah Green, "13 Things You Didn't Know About Queen Esther," Hidabroot: World's Largest Jewish TV Network, https://www.hidabroot.com/article/192836/13-Things-You-Didnt-Know-About-Queen-Esther.

3. Eugene Peterson, *A Long Obedience in the Same Direction: Discipleship in an Instant Society,* (InterVarsity Press, 2019).

4. John Wesley, "Explanatory Notes on Esther 5," accessed March 27, 2019, https://www.christianity.com/bible/commentary.php?com=wes&b=17&c=5.

5. John Wesley, "Explanatory Notes on Esther 5," accessed March 27, 2019, https://www.christianity.com/bible/commentary.php?com=wes&b=17&c=5.

Esther 6: A God We Can Trust

1. Hebrew-Greek Key Word Study Bible, NIV New International Version, 1984 Edition, "read," AMG International Inc, 1996, p. 2009.

2. Esther 6:6, 7, 9, 11 (ESV).

3. Hebrew-Greek Key Word Study Bible, NIV New International Version, 1984 Edition, "been done," AMG International Inc, 1996, p.1995.

4. Cambridge Bible for Schools and Colleges, "Commentary on Esther 6:12," accessed April 3, 2019, https://biblehub.com/commentaries/esther/6-12.htm.

5. Matthew Henry, "Bible Commentary (concise): Esther 6," Christianity.com, https://www.christianity.com/bible/commentary.php?com=mhc&b=17&c=6.

6. Hebrew-Greek Key Word Study Bible, NIV New International Version, 1984 Edition, "will surely come to ruin," AMG International Inc, 1996, p. 1980.

Esther 7: A Foreshadow of the Gospel

1. Hebrew-Greek Key Word Study Bible, NIV New International Version, 1984 Edition, "wicked," AMG International Inc, 1996, p.2014.

2. Hebrew-Greek Key Word Study Bible, NIV New International Version, 1984 Edition, "fell upon," AMG International Inc, 1996, p. 1980.

Esther 9: The Truest Reality

1. Dr. S.M. Lockridge, "That's My King" (sermon), Detroit, Michigan, 1976.

Esther 10: Conclusion

1. Joseph Tenney, "The Greatest Victory", *Raised Sermon Series*, Church at the Cross, June 9, 2019, available on Church at the Cross website, https://churchatthecross.com/raised.